HOW IT WORKS

AF235285

PREHISTORY

ROBERT MUIR-WOOD

award

Series editor: Elizabeth Miles
Cover design: Duck Egg Blue
Illustrations: Jim Channell (Bernard Thornton Artists), Gary Hincks, Stuart Lafford,
Shane Marsh, Sebastian Quigley (Linden Artists), Denys Ovenden, Mike Saunders, Steve Weston
Photography: Joshua Sherurcij, Mai Seppel (Creative Commons 4.0), Shutterstock.com (ajfi, Aunt Spray,
Borislav Bajkic, brandonht, Brian Lasenby, Breck P. Kent, CatbirdHill, DM7, Eva Kali, Geoff Hardy,
Kevin Wells Photography, Lizard, Marques, Michael C. Gray, Mikado767, Nik Keevil, Pablo Caridad,
Phillip Minnis, Procy, Puwadol Jaturawutthichai, Rattana, Rebus_Productions, ruiztome, solarseven,
The Nott'm Lass, Tyler Boyes , worldswildlifewonders, Yurchyks, Zolla Chen, Zoltan Pataki)

ISBN 978-1-78270-008-1

This edition first published 2026

Published by Award Publications Limited,
The Old Riding School, Welbeck, Worksop, S80 3LR

 awardpublications @award.books
www.awardpublications.co.uk

26-1217 1

Printed in China

Contents

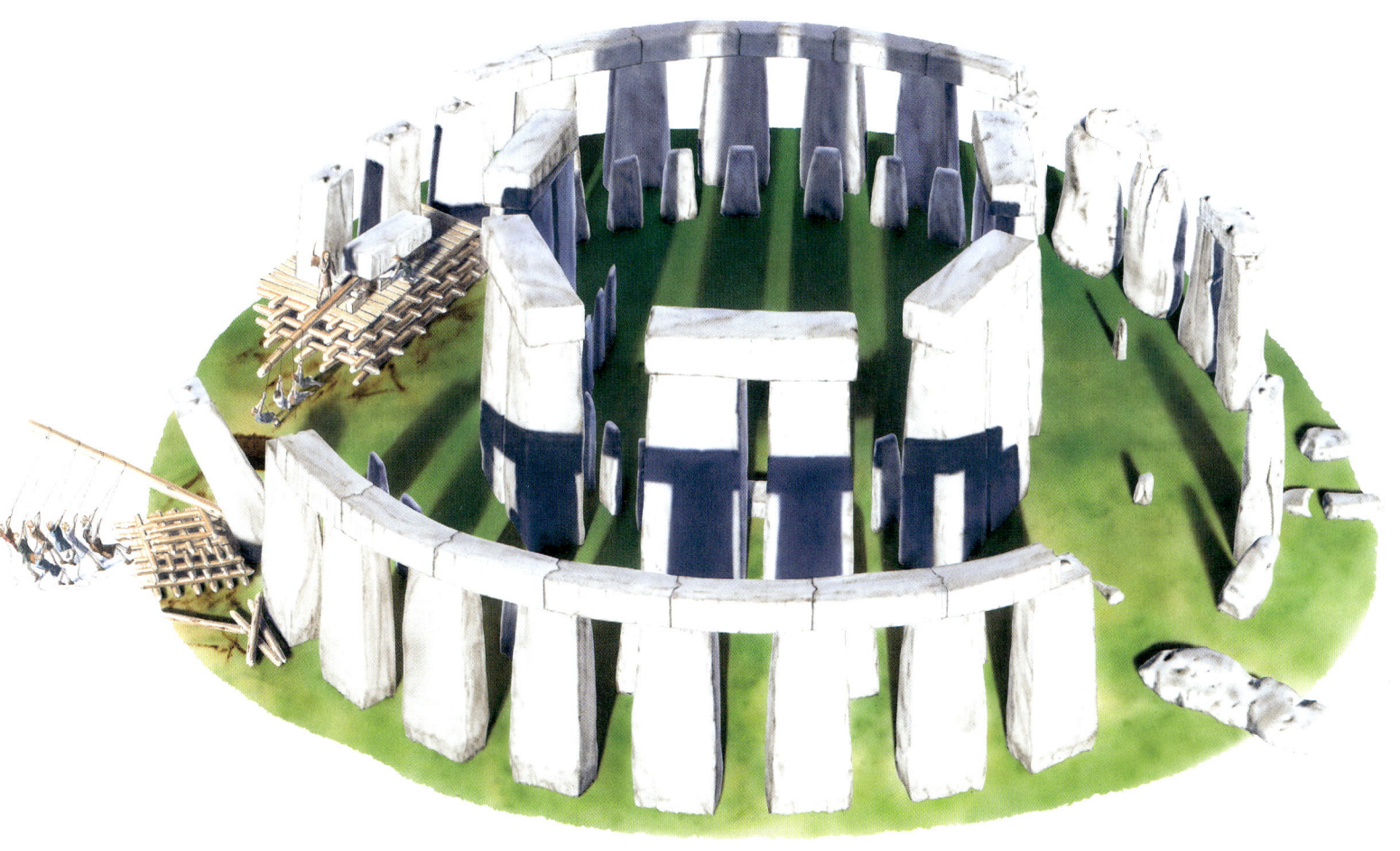

What is Prehistory?

How old is Earth? Have the continents always been the same as they are today? How are mountains formed? How do we know about dinosaurs? Where did the first people come from? To answer these questions we have to explore prehistory.

Prehistory means before history – that is, before our earliest written records, which go back about 4,000 years. Prehistory covers a much longer period – billions of years of deep time. To explore prehistory we need the skills of a detective, searching for clues preserved in the Earth.

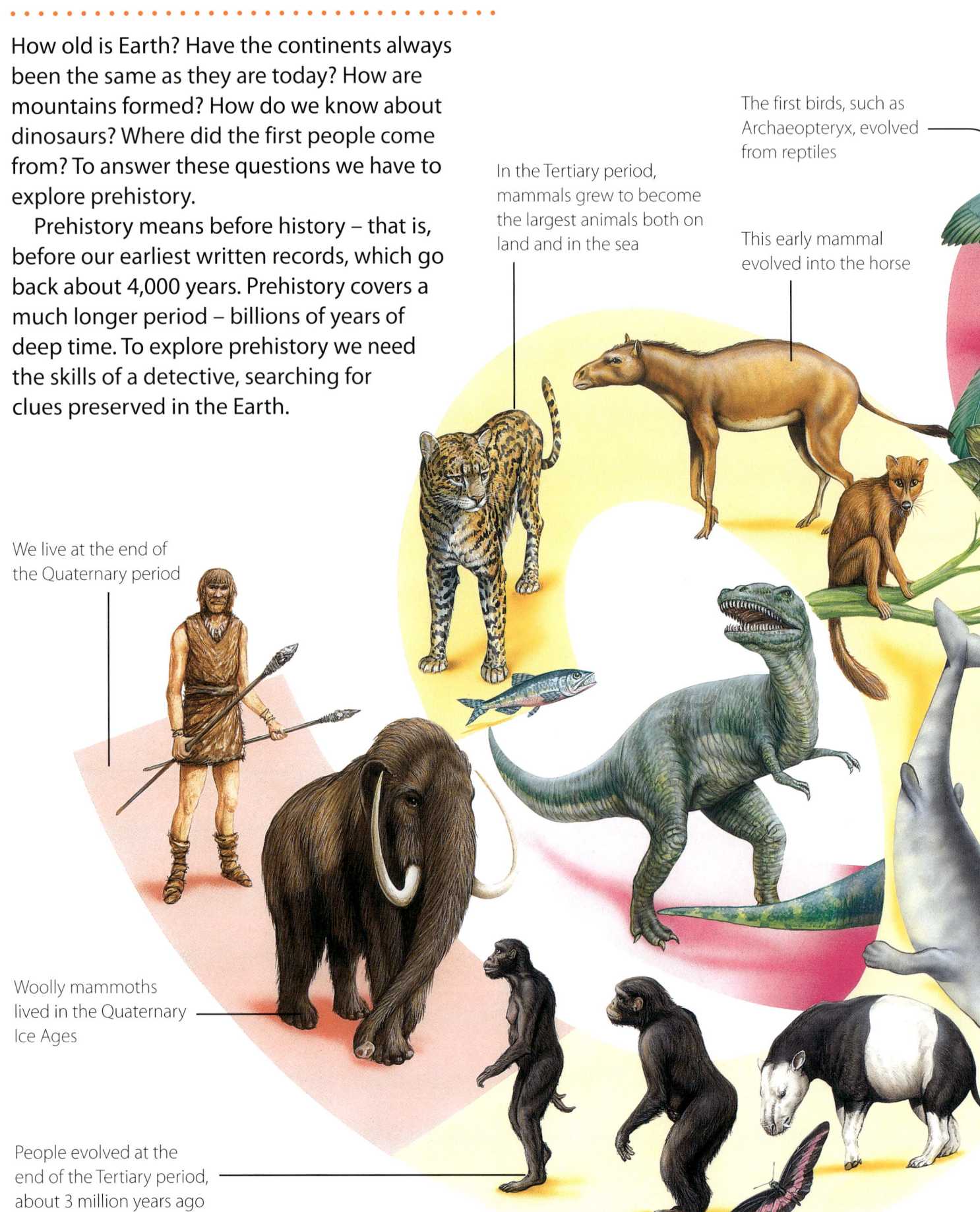

The first birds, such as Archaeopteryx, evolved from reptiles

In the Tertiary period, mammals grew to become the largest animals both on land and in the sea

This early mammal evolved into the horse

We live at the end of the Quaternary period

Woolly mammoths lived in the Quaternary Ice Ages

People evolved at the end of the Tertiary period, about 3 million years ago

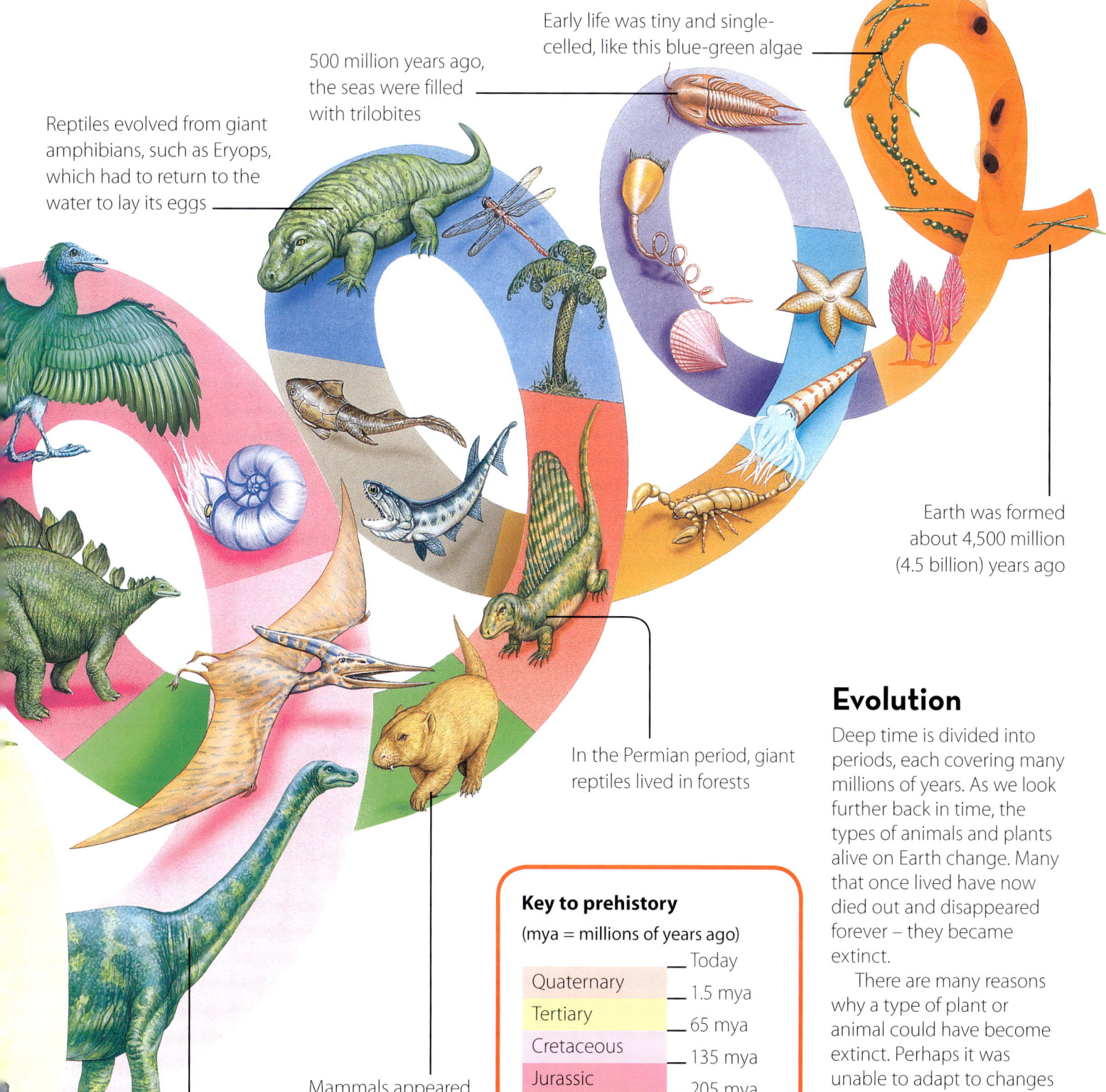

Early life was tiny and single-celled, like this blue-green algae

500 million years ago, the seas were filled with trilobites

Reptiles evolved from giant amphibians, such as Eryops, which had to return to the water to lay its eggs

Earth was formed about 4,500 million (4.5 billion) years ago

In the Permian period, giant reptiles lived in forests

Mammals appeared in the Triassic period

Most dinosaurs lived in the Cretaceous, Jurassic and Triassic periods

Whales are mammals that evolved from land animals no larger than bears

Key to prehistory

(mya = millions of years ago)

	Today
Quaternary	1.5 mya
Tertiary	65 mya
Cretaceous	135 mya
Jurassic	205 mya
Triassic	250 mya
Permian	290 mya
Carboniferous	355 mya
Devonian	410 mya
Silurian	440 mya
Ordovician	510 mya
Cambrian	570 mya
Precambrian	4,500 mya

Evolution

Deep time is divided into periods, each covering many millions of years. As we look further back in time, the types of animals and plants alive on Earth change. Many that once lived have now died out and disappeared forever – they became extinct.

There are many reasons why a type of plant or animal could have become extinct. Perhaps it was unable to adapt to changes in the environment or climate. Perhaps another animal or plant was better suited to the local environment. Plants and animals that do survive adapt to their changing surroundings over many generations and millions of years. The ways in which animals or plants adapt, or change, is called evolution.

Digging Up the Past

To uncover the past, we have to dig down into the earth. Sometimes, rivers have done much of the work by cutting gorges into the land. In Arizona, USA, the Colorado River has cut a gorge down through more than a kilometre of rock. This gorge, called the Grand Canyon, shows a spectacular section of the prehistoric past. Walking to the bottom of the Grand Canyon is like going back in time: the layers of rock around you, and the fossils found within them, are older the further down you go.

Sediment formed over the past 250 million years has been worn away

A simple rule of sediment: younger layers are found on top of older ones

Kaibab limestone (250 million years old)

Coconino sandstone (290 million years old)

Hermit shale (350 million years old)

Fossils of fish scales are found in this layer, which is 390 million years old

Bright Angel shale (530 million years old)

The rocks here are much older and have tilted during the formation of mountains

How the layers formed

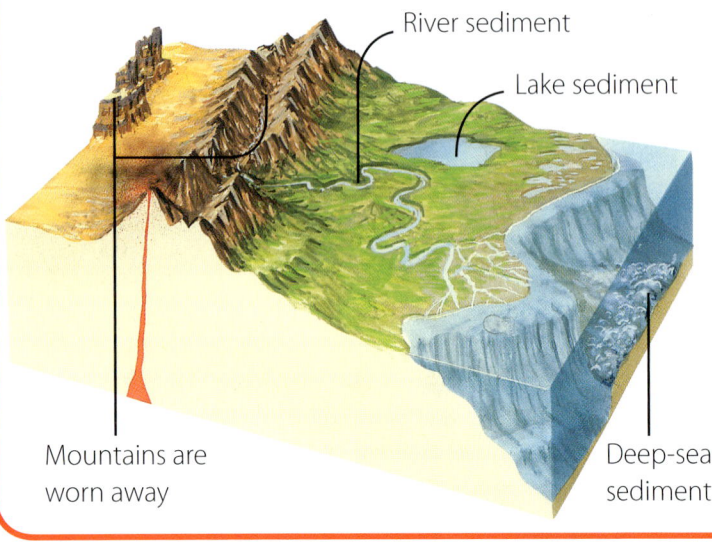

River sediment

Lake sediment

Mountains are worn away

Deep-sea sediment

Mountains are continually being worn down. Fragments of the mountain are worn away and carried off by ice, water and wind, then settle on low land or beneath the water of lakes and seas. These deposits are called sediment. Over millions of years, layers of sediment pile up and harden, forming sedimentary rocks.

These rocks formed 1,700 million years ago, when the only life on Earth was tiny single-celled organisms

The river cuts down through the canyon rocks

Fossils in layers

The age of a layer of sediment is known from the fossils found within it (*see pages 10–11*). Fossils are the remains of living things that have been preserved in rock, or the preserved marks they made in their environment, such as footprints (*see left*). As a result of evolution, living things have slowly changed over time. Fossils show the different life forms that have lived in each period of prehistory. Here, some of the layers of rock that contain fossils are shown enlarged.

Kaibab limestone

Near the top of the Grand Canyon is a layer of Kaibab limestone (**1**) and sandstone. This was deposited in a shallow sea 250 million years ago and is filled with the fossil shells of sea creatures, such as ammonites.

Coconino sandstone

Coconino sandstone sediment (**2**) was laid down on land about 290 million years ago. It contains the footprints of primitive reptiles and amphibians that lived before the dinosaurs.

Hermit shale

Below the sandstone is Hermit shale (**3**). Laid down around 350 million years ago in shallow pools, these mudstones contain raindrop prints and the fossils of insects and ferns.

Bright Angel shale

Bright Angel shale (**4**) was deposited when there were no plants or animals on land. Fossils include trilobites, shells and the burrowing marks of sea creatures that lived 530 million years ago.

How Fossils Form

Fossils have taught us most of what we know about prehistoric plants and animals. They are the traces of past life preserved in rock. Most are formed from the hard parts of animals and plants, but fossils can also record marks such as an animal's footprint left in sand. In order for something to become fossilised it must be buried in sediment quickly before it starts to decay or be worn away. As new layers of sediment are deposited on top, the lower layers become squashed, or compressed. Eventually, over millions of years, these compressed layers turn into rock, and the animal or plant fragments within are preserved in the form of fossils.

Delicate plant material only stays in one piece if it is covered with mud or stagnant water

Only when an animal is suddenly covered in sediment, perhaps in a volcanic eruption, will its bones stay together

Mountains are continually worn away by the weather

Tiny fragments of rock (sediment) are carried by the river to the sea

A big volcanic eruption may deposit a thick layer of ash, which could preserve the bodies of plants and animals

An ammonite fossil

Fossils

Few fossils are made of the original material of a plant or animal. Usually, the material dissolves away, and the hole that is left forms a mould. The mould is then filled with harder minerals left behind by water moving through the surrounding rock, preserving the original shape. The fossils shown here are of an ammonite and an ancient forest fern.

A fossilised leaf

Footprints can only be fossilised if they are quickly covered with sediment

The flesh of a dead dinosaur provides food for other animals, which leave the bones

The bones of a dead dinosaur are covered by sediment

As the river slows, sediment settles on the river bed

Coal is made up of the fossils of leaves and stems of ancient forest plants

When buried, bones may dissolve away and be replaced by minerals to form fossils

11

Comparing Evidence

No single place on Earth can give us a complete record of prehistory. Parts of the record are found scattered in different areas of the world. To link these fragments together, we have to find materials that were formed in different places but at the same time. This process of comparing objects is called correlation. We can also date layers in the soil by correlating objects made by people. For example, we know that bronze was not used by people until about 5,000 years ago. So wherever a bronze item is found, we know the soil it was found in is not more than 5,000 years old.

Correlation between sites

These two excavation sites in Denmark (*on the left*) and Greece (*on the right*) are 900 miles (1,500 kilometres) apart. Sediment carried by rivers and the wind was laid down at both sites over thousands of years. A number of objects and fossils have been found that allow the different layers of sediment to be correlated and dated.

Some soft drink containers are so universal, they can be correlated across the world

Stone to metal

One form of correlation uses objects made by early peoples. The first tools and arrowheads, made from flint and other stone (**I**), were made to a similar design for tens of thousands of years.

The first carved figures (**2**) date from around 30,000 years ago. By 10,000 BC, people had started to fire pottery jars and cups. They travelled long distances and exchanged new ideas with other peoples.

Around 3000 BC, the discovery of bronze led to new types of ornaments being made (**3**). And with the invention of iron smelting around 1000 BC, more effective weapons were possible (**4**). So when we find an iron weapon, we know it must date from after 1000 BC.

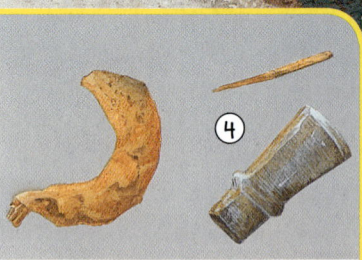

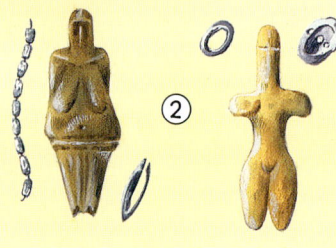

Fragments of iron tools and weapons, 2,500 years old, were found in this layer at both sites

Not all objects are the same everywhere – the designs on pottery, for example, vary from region to region

The discovery of bronze objects means the layer is less than 5,000 years old

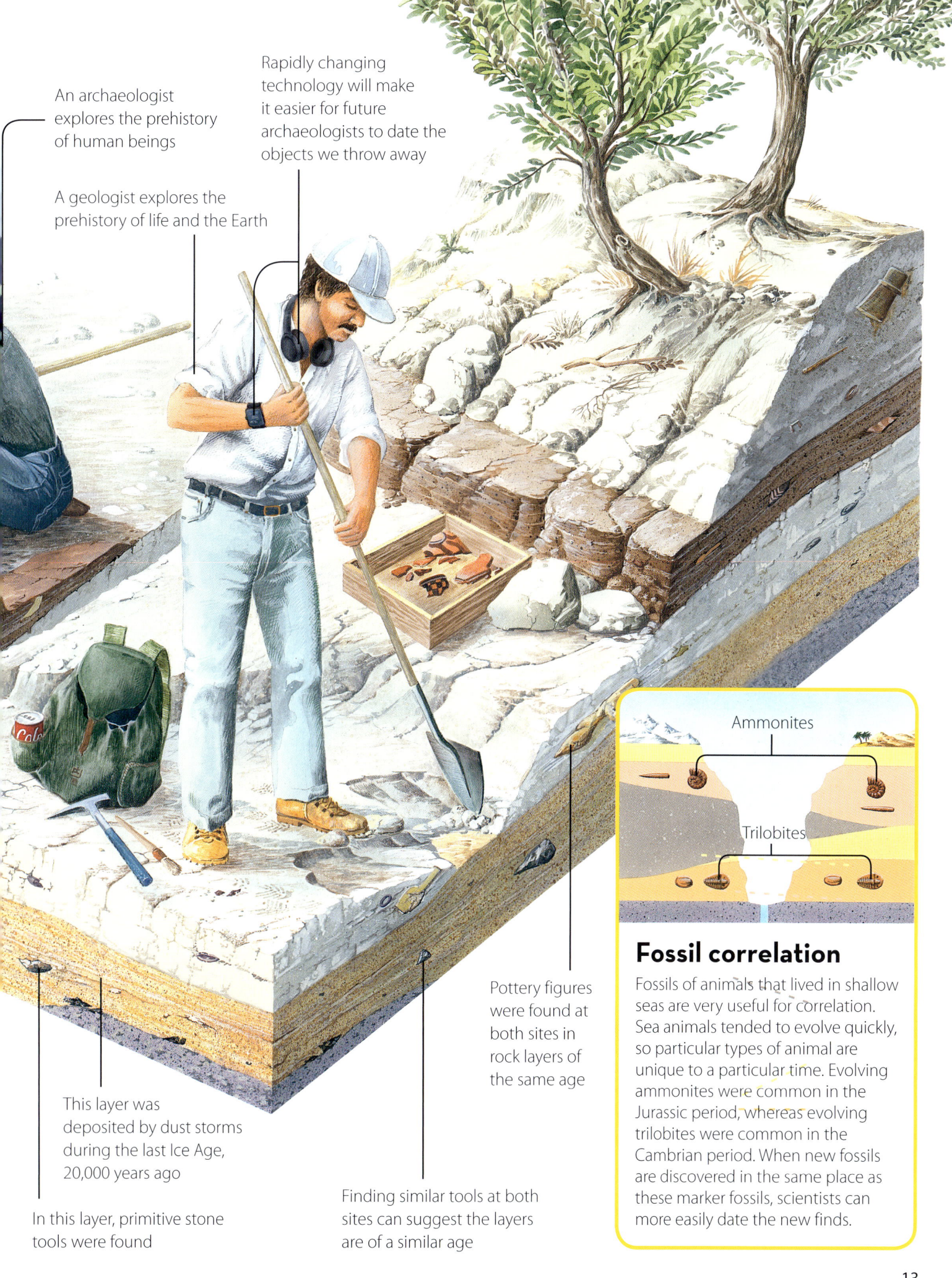

An archaeologist explores the prehistory of human beings

A geologist explores the prehistory of life and the Earth

Rapidly changing technology will make it easier for future archaeologists to date the objects we throw away

This layer was deposited by dust storms during the last Ice Age, 20,000 years ago

In this layer, primitive stone tools were found

Finding similar tools at both sites can suggest the layers are of a similar age

Pottery figures were found at both sites in rock layers of the same age

Ammonites

Trilobites

Fossil correlation

Fossils of animals that lived in shallow seas are very useful for correlation. Sea animals tended to evolve quickly, so particular types of animal are unique to a particular time. Evolving ammonites were common in the Jurassic period, whereas evolving trilobites were common in the Cambrian period. When new fossils are discovered in the same place as these marker fossils, scientists can more easily date the new finds.

Continuous Cores

Some parts of nature hold secrets of their age within them. In the same way that we can follow the evolution of the Earth by digging into it, we can study the layers in the wood of a tree or the ice of an ice sheet. Taking out a core sample from a tree or an ice sheet allows us to count the years back into the past and see a record of changes in the pattern of the weather, which can be compared (correlated) with other cores from around the globe.

Tree cores

Trees do most of their growing in the summer. If a tree trunk is cut across its width, you can see a pattern of rings: wider bands of spring early wood, separated by narrow, darker bands of autumn and winter late wood. Changes in climate alter the widths of the rings from year to year. By studying the ring patterns and matching them against older tree cores, we can learn how the climate has changed over thousands of years.

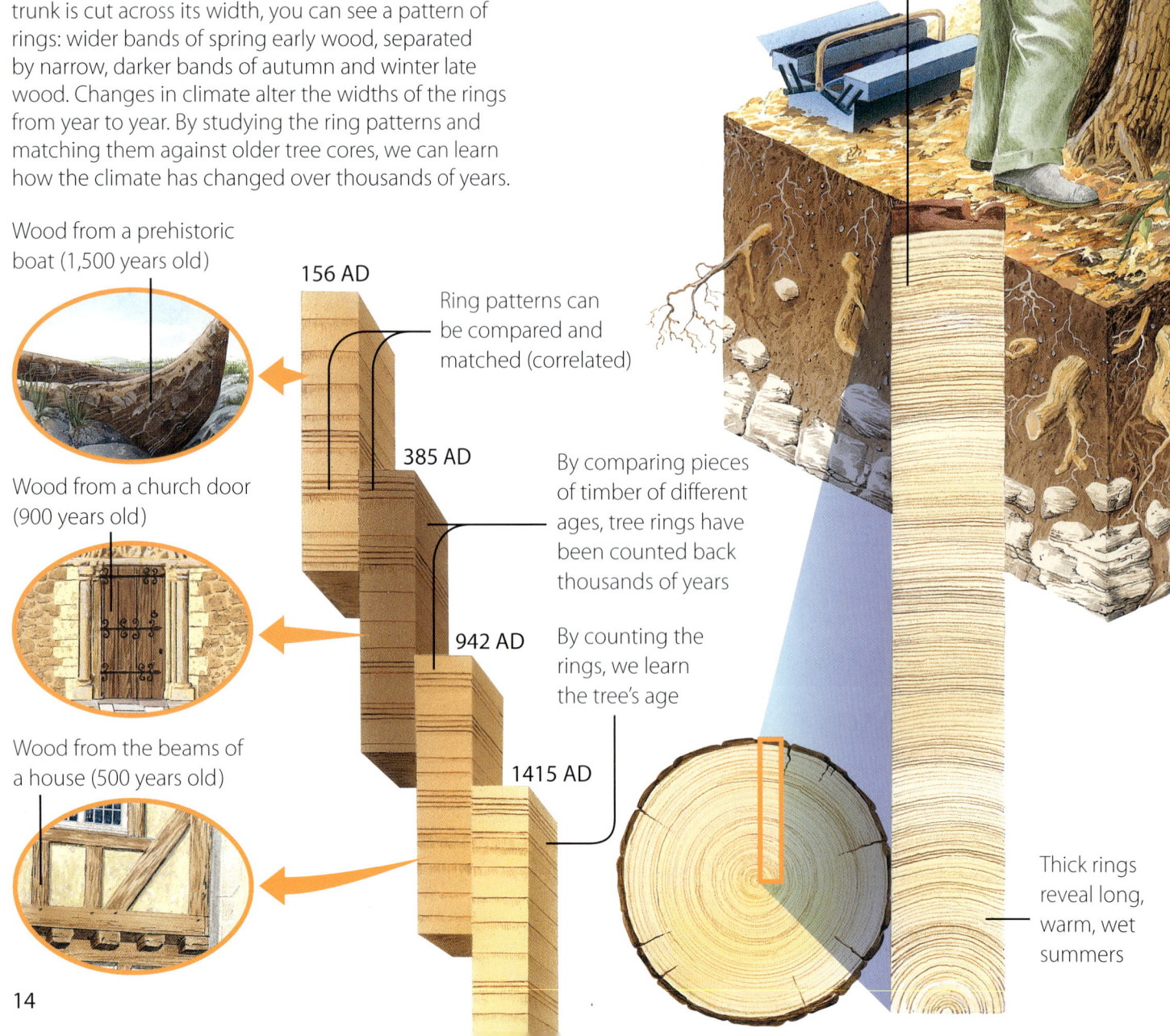

Using a narrow corer, it is possible to obtain a continuous section through a living tree without damaging it

A core taken from the centre of a living tree

Wood from a prehistoric boat (1,500 years old)

156 AD

Ring patterns can be compared and matched (correlated)

385 AD

By comparing pieces of timber of different ages, tree rings have been counted back thousands of years

Wood from a church door (900 years old)

942 AD

By counting the rings, we learn the tree's age

1415 AD

Wood from the beams of a house (500 years old)

Thick rings reveal long, warm, wet summers

14

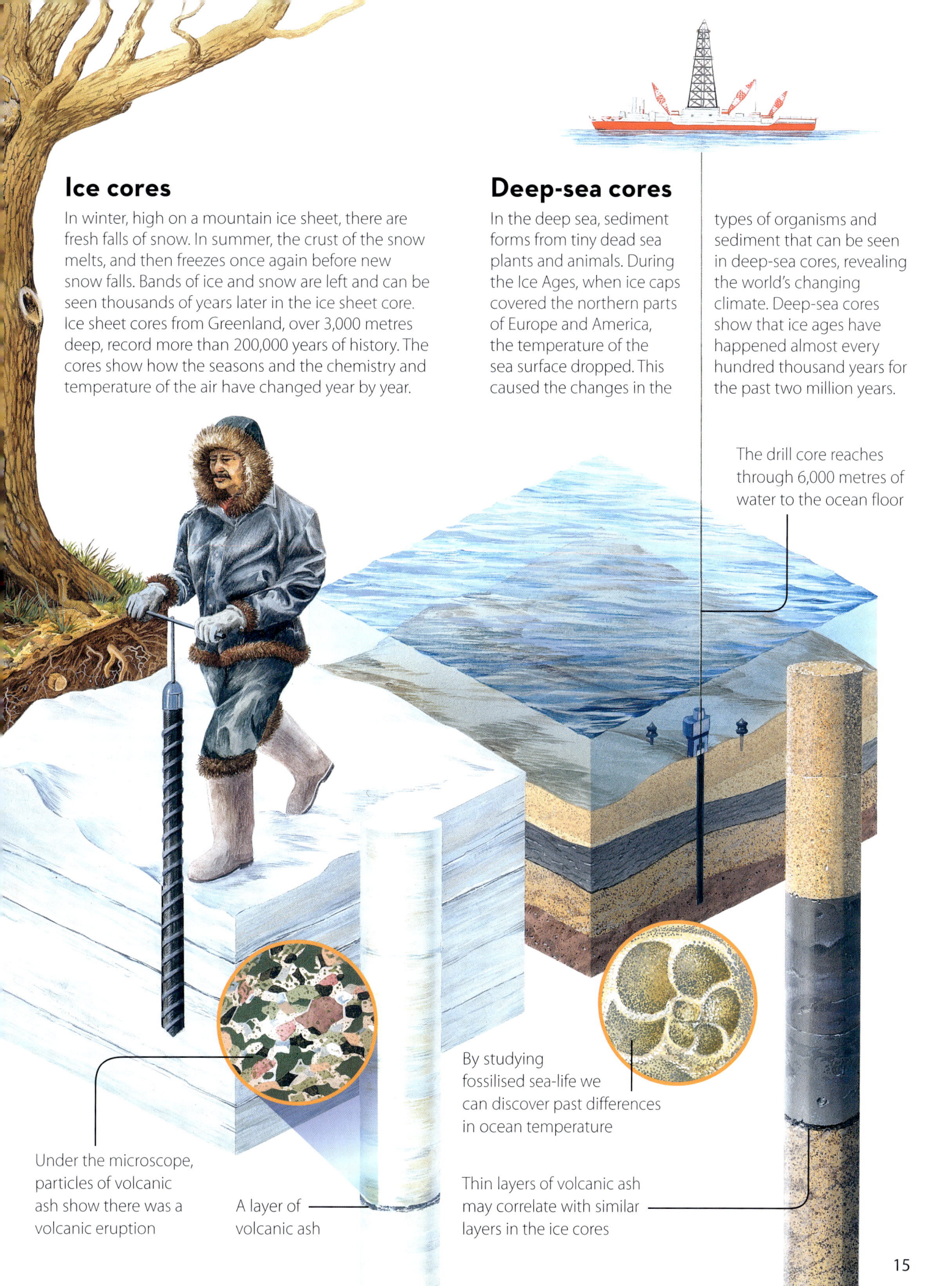

Ice cores

In winter, high on a mountain ice sheet, there are fresh falls of snow. In summer, the crust of the snow melts, and then freezes once again before new snow falls. Bands of ice and snow are left and can be seen thousands of years later in the ice sheet core. Ice sheet cores from Greenland, over 3,000 metres deep, record more than 200,000 years of history. The cores show how the seasons and the chemistry and temperature of the air have changed year by year.

Deep-sea cores

In the deep sea, sediment forms from tiny dead sea plants and animals. During the Ice Ages, when ice caps covered the northern parts of Europe and America, the temperature of the sea surface dropped. This caused the changes in the types of organisms and sediment that can be seen in deep-sea cores, revealing the world's changing climate. Deep-sea cores show that ice ages have happened almost every hundred thousand years for the past two million years.

The drill core reaches through 6,000 metres of water to the ocean floor

By studying fossilised sea-life we can discover past differences in ocean temperature

Under the microscope, particles of volcanic ash show there was a volcanic eruption

A layer of volcanic ash

Thin layers of volcanic ash may correlate with similar layers in the ice cores

Counting Radioisotopes

The years of deep time can be charted in rocks. Rocks contain radioisotopes – atoms that are unstable and fall apart (decay) at a constant rate. A large number of these radioisotope atoms slowly change from parent atoms to daughter atoms. The age of a rock can be found by measuring how many of the parent atoms have decayed into daughter atoms. For some radioisotopes, millions of years will pass before they have all become daughter atoms.

The radioisotope of the element potassium is useful for dating prehistory because it is found in many ancient rocks. The parent atom potassium decays into the daughter atom argon. By counting the radioisotopes using instruments such as Geiger counters, we can find the age of ancient rocks that are sometimes billions of years old. Radioisotope dating provides a calendar of prehistory, helping us to reconstruct the past.

Volcanic rocks

Volcanic rocks (I), or lava, often contain potassium-rich minerals. By counting the radioisotopes we can tell when the volcano erupted. This could help us date the fossils of dinosaurs that died in the red-hot lava.

Ⓘ

Dating this rock shows the volcano erupted 250 million years ago

One potassium atom has become an argon atom

Lava (molten rock from the volcano) runs across the land

Meteorite crater

Lava cools and solidifies over the animals's remains

Its fossil shows that that *Dimetrodon* died in the eruption

Trilobite fossils

A layer of sedimentary rock

Rocks from this prehistoric scene could be found today and dated

16

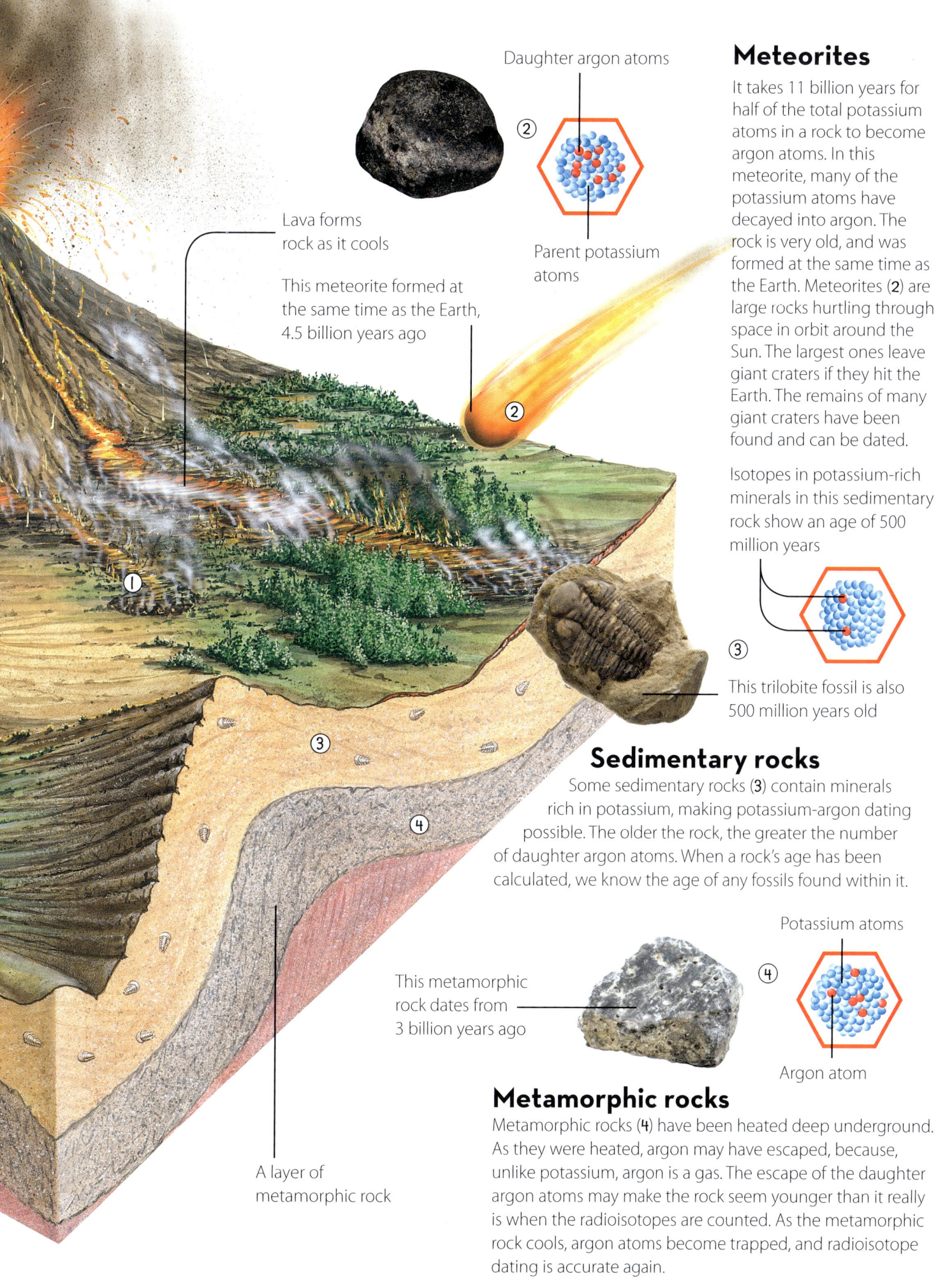

Lava forms
rock as it cools

This meteorite formed at
the same time as the Earth,
4.5 billion years ago

Daughter argon atoms

②

Parent potassium
atoms

Meteorites

It takes 11 billion years for
half of the total potassium
atoms in a rock to become
argon atoms. In this
meteorite, many of the
potassium atoms have
decayed into argon. The
rock is very old, and was
formed at the same time as
the Earth. Meteorites (**2**) are
large rocks hurtling through
space in orbit around the
Sun. The largest ones leave
giant craters if they hit the
Earth. The remains of many
giant craters have been
found and can be dated.

Isotopes in potassium-rich
minerals in this sedimentary
rock show an age of 500
million years

③

This trilobite fossil is also
500 million years old

Sedimentary rocks

Some sedimentary rocks (**3**) contain minerals
rich in potassium, making potassium-argon dating
possible. The older the rock, the greater the number
of daughter argon atoms. When a rock's age has been
calculated, we know the age of any fossils found within it.

Potassium atoms

④

Argon atom

This metamorphic
rock dates from
3 billion years ago

A layer of
metamorphic rock

Metamorphic rocks

Metamorphic rocks (**4**) have been heated deep underground.
As they were heated, argon may have escaped, because,
unlike potassium, argon is a gas. The escape of the daughter
argon atoms may make the rock seem younger than it really
is when the radioisotopes are counted. As the metamorphic
rock cools, argon atoms become trapped, and radioisotope
dating is accurate again.

Radiocarbon Dating

Radiocarbon (or carbon-14) dating gives archaeologists an accurate age of material that was once living, such as plants and animals. While radioisotope dating can be used for measuring rocks that have been around since the formation of the Earth, radiocarbon dating can only be used for dating material from the past 40,000 years.

Carbon-14 is a radioactive form of the element carbon that is continually being created at the top of Earth's atmosphere. Carbon is taken up by plants. Animals and humans take in carbon-14 when they eat plants and when they breathe. When a plant or animal dies, it no longer takes in carbon-14, but the carbon-14 left in the dead material gradually decays. By measuring the amount left in the material, archaeologists can tell how long it is since the organism died.

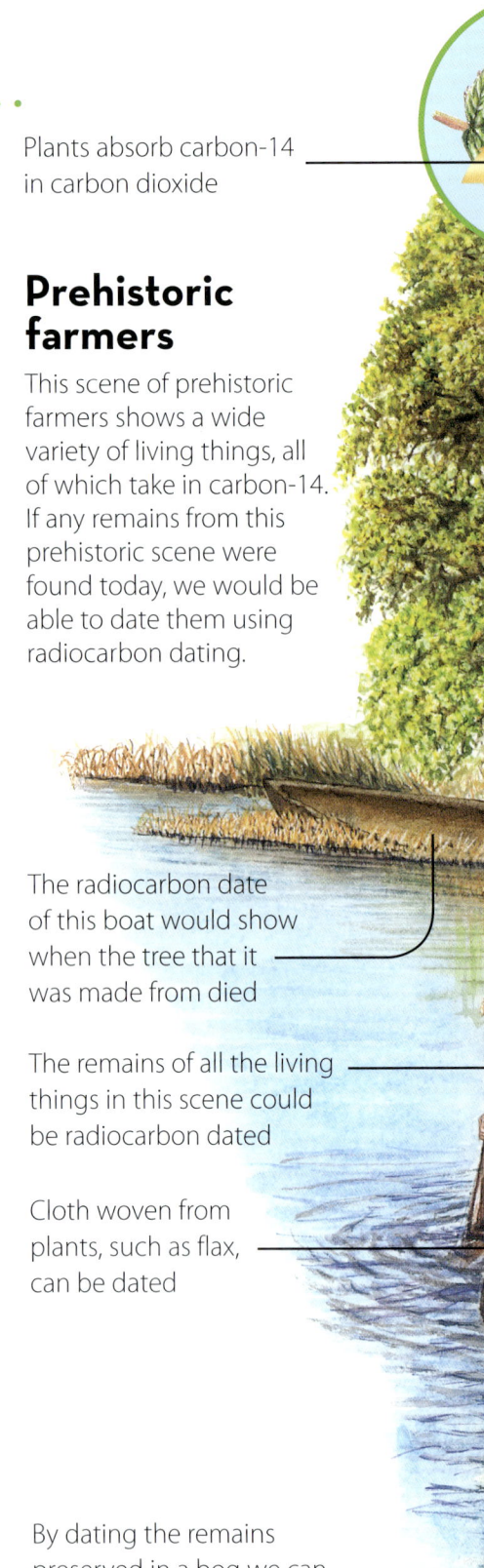

Plants absorb carbon-14 in carbon dioxide

Prehistoric farmers

This scene of prehistoric farmers shows a wide variety of living things, all of which take in carbon-14. If any remains from this prehistoric scene were found today, we would be able to date them using radiocarbon dating.

The radiocarbon date of this boat would show when the tree that it was made from died

The remains of all the living things in this scene could be radiocarbon dated

Cloth woven from plants, such as flax, can be dated

By dating the remains preserved in a bog we can reconstruct a scene like this from 2,500 years ago

Carbon-14

2,500 years ago

2,000 years ago

Today

When a tree is cut down, it dies and stops taking in carbon-14 from the atmosphere. The tree might be made into a boat, but the carbon-14 in the wood would continue to decay. After 5,730 years, half the carbon-14 will have gone. After 11,460 years, only a quarter will be left. Pictured (*left*) is a boat that was made by prehistoric farmers. Buried in the soil, it gradually decayed. Radiocarbon dating of a piece of the boat today might show it as being 2,500 years old, with more than a quarter of its carbon-14 gone.

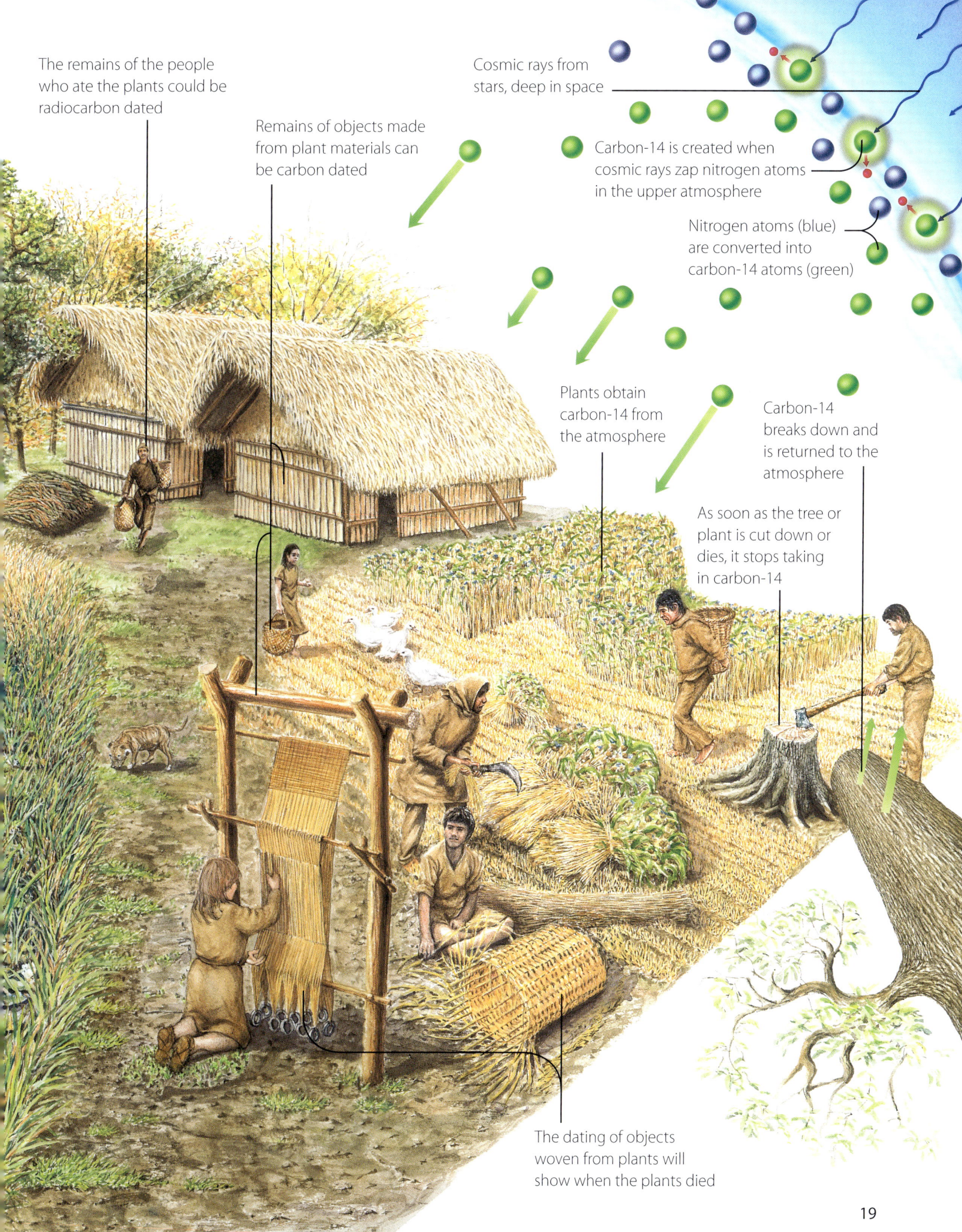

The remains of the people who ate the plants could be radiocarbon dated

Remains of objects made from plant materials can be carbon dated

Cosmic rays from stars, deep in space

Carbon-14 is created when cosmic rays zap nitrogen atoms in the upper atmosphere

Nitrogen atoms (blue) are converted into carbon-14 atoms (green)

Plants obtain carbon-14 from the atmosphere

Carbon-14 breaks down and is returned to the atmosphere

As soon as the tree or plant is cut down or dies, it stops taking in carbon-14

The dating of objects woven from plants will show when the plants died

Dinosaur Excavation

Important fossil finds must be dug out, or excavated, very carefully. The first discovery may be the chance sighting of a fossil sticking out of a cliff or the glimpse of a bone as the foundations of a new building are being dug. Unlike most fossil discoveries, this dinosaur skeleton is complete. The animal died and was preserved all in one place. Finds like this are very rare and demand the most careful excavation to ensure that nothing is broken and nothing is missed. To help rebuild the skeleton accurately, scientists have to record the position of every tiny fragment of bone.

The site is excavated layer by layer – a pickaxe is used to break up the top layer of rock

The exact location of all the bones is recorded using a grid

A groove is carefully cut round the bone with a hammer and chisel

Sieves are used to catch small fragments of the skeleton

Fragile bones are cleaned with a paintbrush

The skull of the dinosaur is already being freed

Bones are wrapped in fabric strips dipped in plaster of Paris

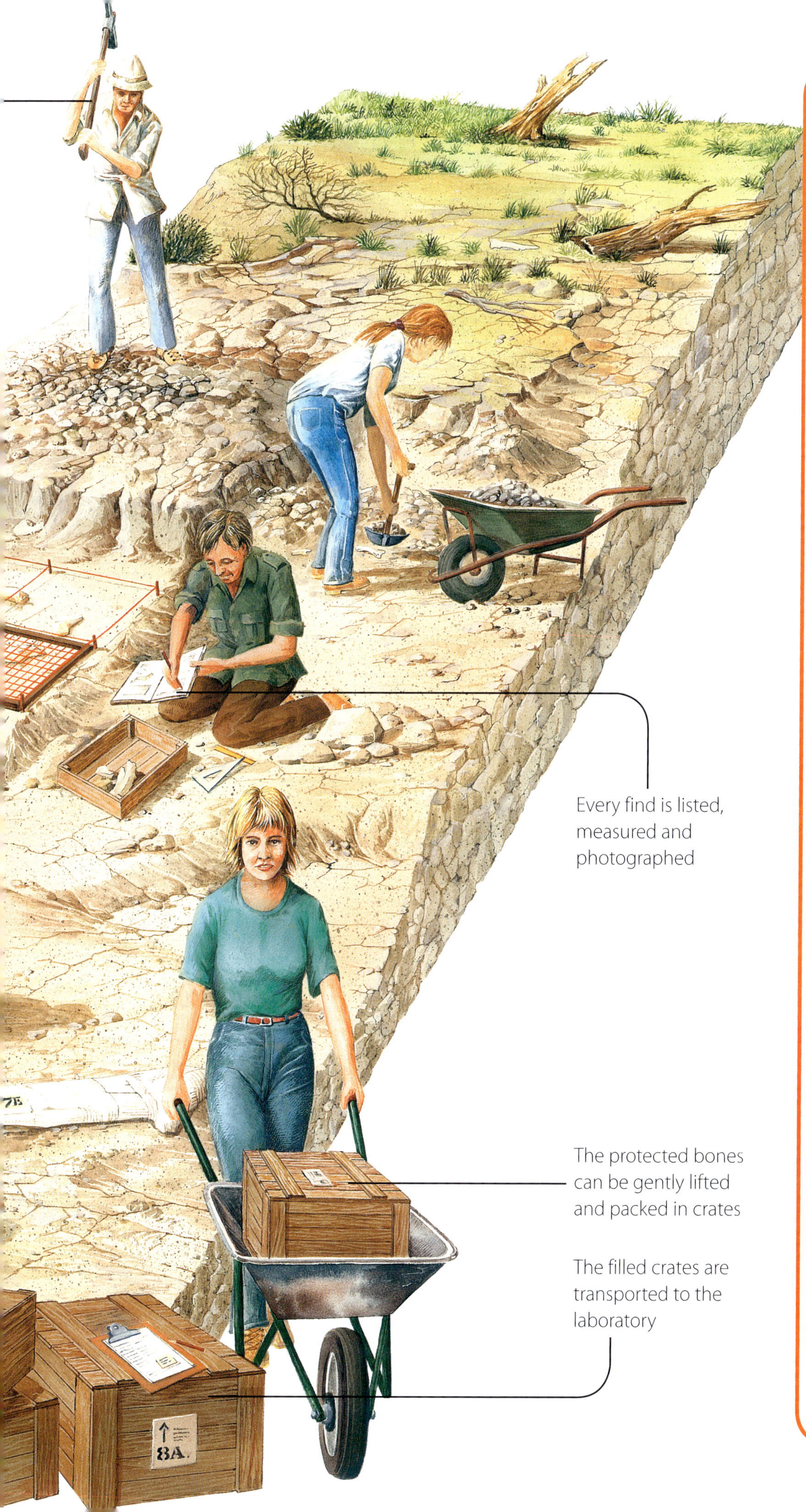

In the laboratory

The jawbone is the strongest part of a skull and may be the only piece to survive. How much the teeth have been worn down can reveal the animal's age when it died and the sorts of food it ate.

The jawbone arrives in the laboratory in its protective covering. This is removed and any stone left on it is dissolved with weak acid.

Detailed cleaning is carried out using various fine instruments, like a dentist's drill or a small chisel. The cleaned bone fragments are then carefully examined to see how they fitted together.

The fragments are scanned in 3D. Teeth can be put back into the jawbone and glued into place. Any missing pieces of bone or teeth can be replaced by plaster or 3D printed materials. The scans can also be studied by researchers using 3D modelling software and used to reconstruct models of the dinosaur's skeleton and body.

Every find is listed, measured and photographed

The protected bones can be gently lifted and packed in crates

The filled crates are transported to the laboratory

Dinosaur Reconstruction

What did dinosaurs look like? The bones show us the skeleton, but to know what the dinosaur actually looked like, it is necessary to model it, by adding muscles and skin. The first stage – putting a dinosaur skeleton together – is like solving a jigsaw puzzle, but some of the pieces may be missing and others broken. However, there are so many similarities between dinosaurs and animals living today that it is possible to find the right places for almost all the bones, simply by comparing their shapes to those of today's animals. Once the skeleton has been formed, the muscles can be added and then the skin.

The muscles had to be large enough to allow Triceratops to charge at its attackers

The muscles of dinosaurs were similar in shape to those of birds and crocodiles

The pattern of muscles can be reconstructed by working out how the limbs moved

What was the skin like?

Fossilised fragments of dinosaur skin are sometimes found. The fragment above has a pattern similar to that of a lizard's, but on a larger scale. The skin had to be very tough to withstand contact with spiny trees or bushes. The colour of the skin does not show on the fossil. We can only guess at dinosaur colours, but they were probably similar to modern reptile colours.

Triceratops was probably grey, like the modern animal that shares a similar lifestyle – the rhinoceros

The overall shape of the skeleton shows *Triceratops* walked on its toes

Where were the muscles attached?

There are often markings on the bones where large muscles were attached. From these muscle scar markings, it is possible to begin to reconstruct the muscles of the legs and body.

Horns were used as weapons to defend against attack

Missing parts of the fossil are filled in with plaster

Plaster

Missing bones

Many bones in a body are the same as other bones: one rib is very similar to another rib. If a bone is missing, either a copy can be made or it can be reconstructed from those that do exist. Cast in plaster or 3D printed from digital scans, these newly-made bones can be used to complete the skeleton.

Assembling the skeleton

For display in a museum, complete skeletons of fossilised or newly-made bones are gathered and laid out (1).

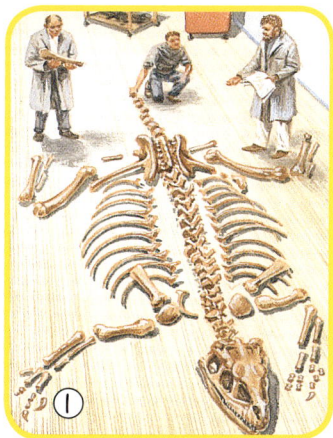

Starting with the spine, the bones are wired together and raised into position on a mount (2).

Computer simulations are used to work out how the dinosaur moved. Each bone is measured, and the data is entered into the computer. The program then 'draws' a three-dimensional model of the dinosaur. It can be moved on-screen to create different life-like poses to enhance museum displays (3).

How the Dinosaurs Lived

What were the dinosaurs like? Did they walk, or could they run fast? How did they fight? What kind of noises did they make? Will we ever know how they lived? Just like any other animal, every part of a dinosaur's body helped it to survive. So every part of a dinosaur that we find tells us something about how it lived.

Some of the most amazing dinosaurs lived alongside each other. *Parasaurolophos* was a duck-billed dinosaur that lived in forests. *Ankylosaurus* was an armoured dinosaur that lived in open grassland. Both habitats were home to the fearsome *Tyrannosaurus rex*, which preyed on both *Ankylosaurus* and *Parasaurolophus*.

A dinosaur's meal

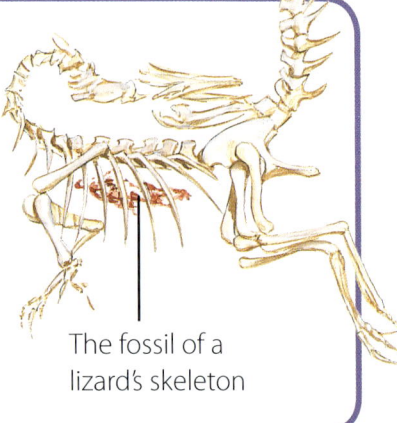

Sometimes, we can even find out what a dinosaur last ate before it died. This *Compsognathus* had just eaten a lizard. The lizard's skeleton was fossilised in the dinosaur's ribcage.

The fossil of a lizard's skeleton

A duck-billed dinosaur

This plant-eating *Parasaurolophos* is called a duck-billed dinosaur because of the crest on its head. The one-metre long crest was partly a colourful ornament to display to other dinosaurs. But it also contained air tubes, which may have given the animal an acute sense of smell.

Hollow air tubes ran through its crest

These teeth were shaped for grinding vegetation

Perhaps the crest was used to make trumpeting noises to attract other *Parasaurolophus*

Dinosaur nest

We know some dinosaurs had nesting colonies, where they laid their eggs together. The remains of some of these colonies have been found in fossilised form. These *Maiasaurus* nests were made of mounds of sand. Fossils of 15 newly-hatched dinosaur babies were found next to one nest.

A meat-eater

The most fearsome of the meat-eating dinosaurs, *Tyrannosaurus rex*, was well adapted for fighting. It grew up to 14 metres long, and its massive jaws (which were themselves as long as 1.4 metres) were filled with dagger-like teeth used for ripping flesh.

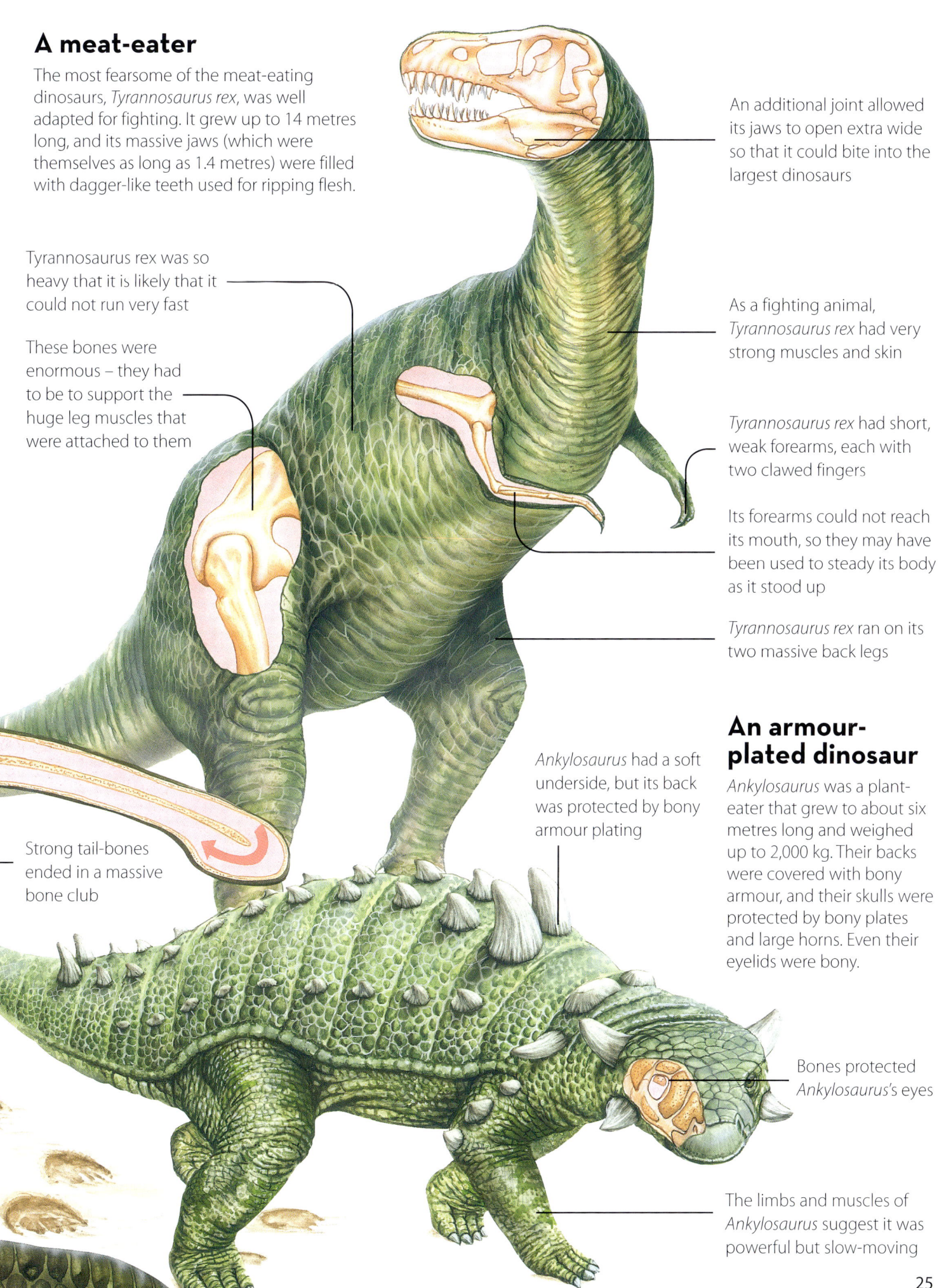

An additional joint allowed its jaws to open extra wide so that it could bite into the largest dinosaurs

Tyrannosaurus rex was so heavy that it is likely that it could not run very fast

These bones were enormous – they had to be to support the huge leg muscles that were attached to them

As a fighting animal, *Tyrannosaurus rex* had very strong muscles and skin

Tyrannosaurus rex had short, weak forearms, each with two clawed fingers

Its forearms could not reach its mouth, so they may have been used to steady its body as it stood up

Tyrannosaurus rex ran on its two massive back legs

Strong tail-bones ended in a massive bone club

Ankylosaurus had a soft underside, but its back was protected by bony armour plating

An armour-plated dinosaur

Ankylosaurus was a plant-eater that grew to about six metres long and weighed up to 2,000 kg. Their backs were covered with bony armour, and their skulls were protected by bony plates and large horns. Even their eyelids were bony.

Bones protected *Ankylosaurus*'s eyes

The limbs and muscles of *Ankylosaurus* suggest it was powerful but slow-moving

25

How the Dinosaurs Died Out

Dinosaurs ruled the Earth for 150 million years. Then, quite suddenly, 65 million years ago, they died out. They were not, however, the only animals to become extinct at this time. Many animals living in the sea also disappeared, along with many varieties of tiny sea-dwelling plants. The remains of these plants and animals settled on the sea and river beds. Over millions of years, these remains formed layers of sedimentary rock. It is this rock which helps us understand why the dinosaurs disappeared. The main cause appears to have been an asteroid that collided with the Earth, causing massive damage. But sediment in the rock suggests other causes, too, such as volcanic activity and climate change.

An asteroid is a mountain-sized boulder from outer space

An asteroid crater like this, measuring 120 miles (200 km) across, is buried beneath the coast of Mexico

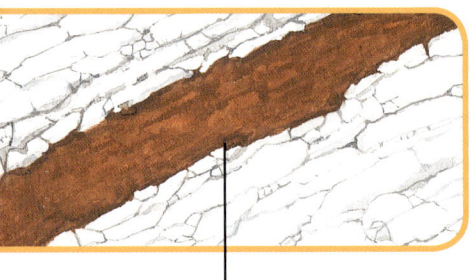

A layer of dark clay between layers of chalk

Death in the sea

A drop in temperature, as a result of thick smoke and dust in the air, could explain why so many animals died out. In many parts of the world, a layer of clay, formed from the remains of sea life, sandwiched between thick layers of chalk shows us the time period when over three quarters of living species became extinct.

Perhaps the Earth's atmosphere became poisoned by clouds of volcanic gas and dust

Forest fires

Tiny particles of burnt wood, or charcoal, have been found in sediment laid down at the time the dinosaurs died out. This charcoal must have come from huge forest fires, perhaps covering millions of square kilometres. Many of the dinosaurs may have perished in the fires and smoke.

A layer rich in charcoal

In western India there were enormous volcanic eruptions at the time the dinosaurs died out

Shocked quartz

An asteroid

Quartz is a mineral found in many rocks. When scientists examined ancient rock formed at the same time that the dinosaurs died out, they found that the quartz's crystal structure was different to normal quartz. This 'shocked' quartz could only have been created by a massive explosion, such as a giant asteroid colliding with the Earth. The impact would have caused a huge dust cloud, reduced the amount of the Sun's heat and light reaching the Earth's surface for months, causing temperatures to drop. Frosts would have killed forests, and many animals would have died.

Shock waves may have started forest fires

An asteroid impact, volcanic pollution (*see photo below*) and climate change may together have wiped out the dinosaurs

After the plant-eaters had died, there would have been no food left for meat-eaters

As the forests were killed by the cold, the first dinosaurs to die were the plant-eaters

Dust clouds from volcanic eruptions can reduce how much heat and light reaches the Earth's surface for months

There must have been a global change in climate, because even the tropics suffered from frosts

Ancient Climates

Climate is the weather observed over many years: how hot, cold, wet and dry it is. Climate affects the type of landscape, plants and animals that are found in a region.

Over millions of years, the climate of the world has changed. At times, there have been great ice sheets over parts of the Earth's surface. At other times, deserts have covered whole continents, and lush rainforest has later grown on these same lands. Great forests have sunk to become lifeless salt lakes, and these in turn have been flooded as the rain returned. The continents have also moved across the globe, passing from one climate region to another. When sediment is laid down, it contains 'climate fossils' – evidence that we can use to reconstruct the type of weather and landscapes that existed in that place millions of years ago.

Different types of sediment are evidence of different climates

Limestone sediment forms in shallow seas

Fossils of sea life

The upper layers of sediment are the youngest; the bottom layers are are the oldest

Dry lakes in deserts leave layers of salty sediment

Fossilised rainforests become thick layers of coal (*see pages 30–31*)

Tilted sandy layers show there were once sand dunes

As glaciers melted, they left thick piles of mud and boulders

Ice age rivers deposited thick sediment in the summer, but little in the winter, when they froze

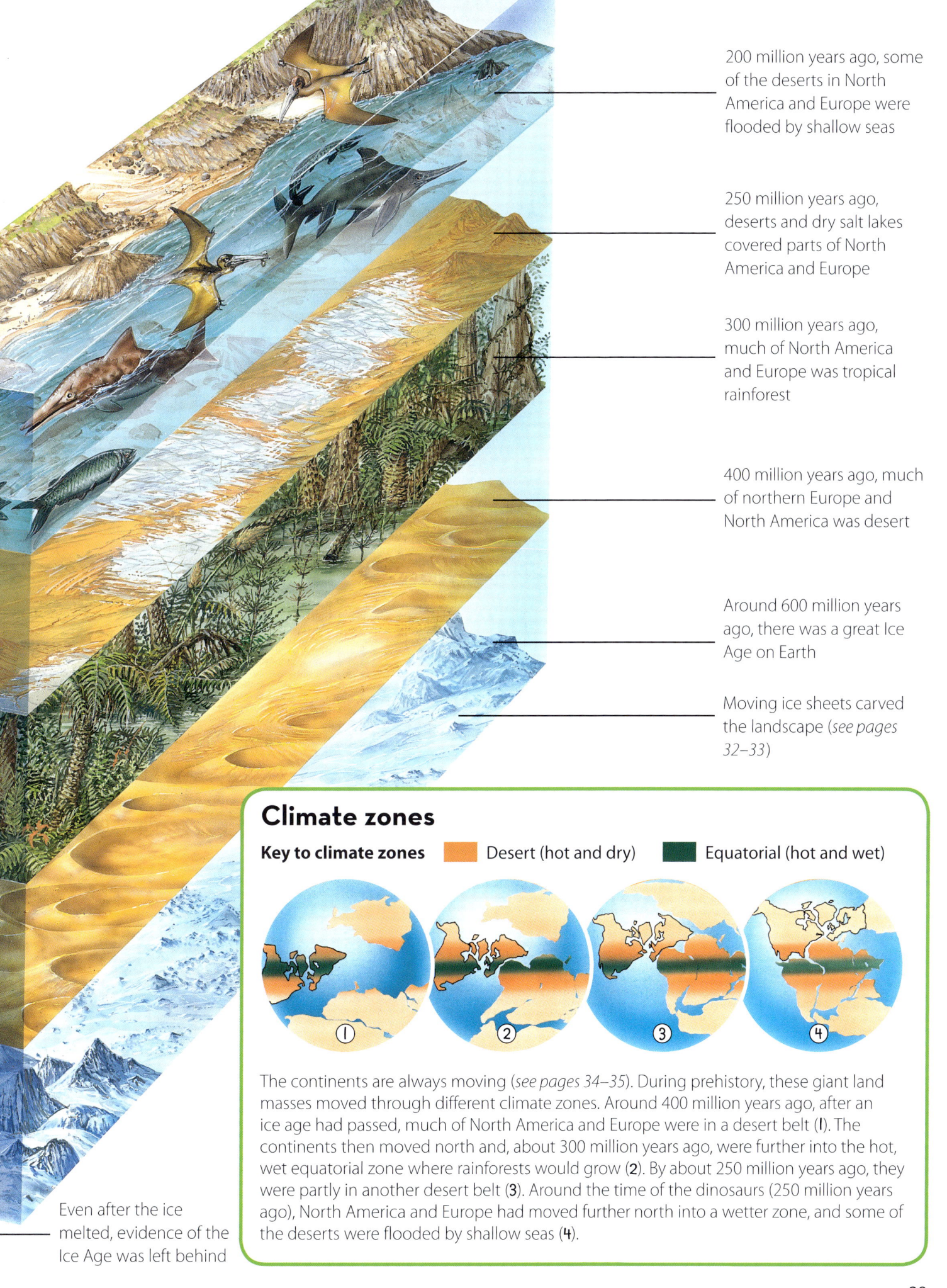

200 million years ago, some of the deserts in North America and Europe were flooded by shallow seas

250 million years ago, deserts and dry salt lakes covered parts of North America and Europe

300 million years ago, much of North America and Europe was tropical rainforest

400 million years ago, much of northern Europe and North America was desert

Around 600 million years ago, there was a great Ice Age on Earth

Moving ice sheets carved the landscape (*see pages 32–33*)

Even after the ice melted, evidence of the Ice Age was left behind

Climate zones

Key to climate zones   ■ Desert (hot and dry)   ■ Equatorial (hot and wet)

①   ②   ③   ④

The continents are always moving (*see pages 34–35*). During prehistory, these giant land masses moved through different climate zones. Around 400 million years ago, after an ice age had passed, much of North America and Europe were in a desert belt (**1**). The continents then moved north and, about 300 million years ago, were further into the hot, wet equatorial zone where rainforests would grow (**2**). By about 250 million years ago, they were partly in another desert belt (**3**). Around the time of the dinosaurs (250 million years ago), North America and Europe had moved further north into a wetter zone, and some of the deserts were flooded by shallow seas (**4**).

Carboniferous Forests

Around 4 billion years ago, the first plants to live on land appeared. They developed from water-living algae. The first tropical rainforests formed about 70 million years later, and in another 50 million years the forests covered enormous areas of lowland. In the forests, plants developed giant, tree-like forms, reaching higher and higher above each other to seek sunlight. Below the treetops, the crowded forests were dark and damp. These forests were similar to today's rainforests, although many of the trees looked very different and there were no birds or monkeys. Instead, in the air and on the forest floor, there were giant insects. There were also large, fish-eating amphibians living in the swamps. We know what lived in these rainforests because many fossils were left behind in the rock we call coal.

Evidence from coal

The first rainforests appeared in the Carboniferous period. When the trees in the early forests died, they sank into a swamp (1). Here, where the land was slowly sinking, rotting leaves and logs gradually formed a damp soil called peat (2). As the layer of peat became covered by more sediment, the water in it was squeezed out.

Over millions of years, more and more water was squeezed out until it became coal. All that we know about the first rainforests has come from studying pieces of coal, the material that is dug from coal mines and burned in some power stations (3).

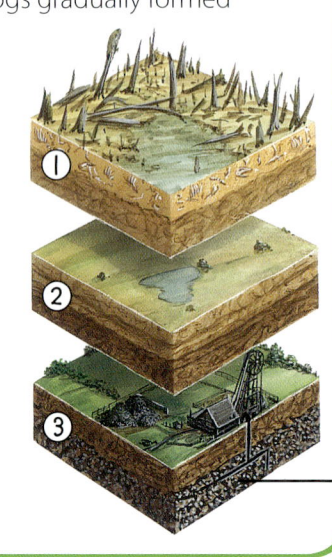

Giant club mosses grew in the swamps

Giant tree ferns

A layer of rotting plant and animal remains

A layer of peat, which slowly turned into coal over millions of years

The coal that is burned in some homes and in coal-fired power stations is the remains of 300-million-year-old rainforests

Giant millipedes, up to two metres long, crawled across the forest floor

Huge dragonflies, with wingspans of up to 70 centimetres, flew through the air

Fossilised tree trunks show that the trees reached heights of 30 metres

This giant club moss is called *Lepidodendron*

Forest fossils

Coal comes from dead plants. Well-preserved fossils of leaves, stems and trunks are often found in coal, although they are always compressed, or squashed. Petrified tree trunks, such as this *Sigillaria* (below) are created when minerals replace the dead tree's organic matter.

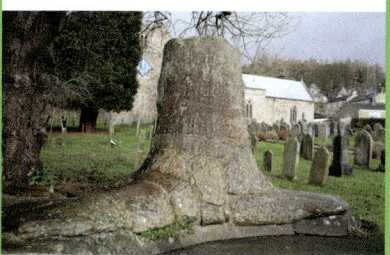

The bark of *Lepidodendron*, a giant club moss, had overlapping scales (*below left*). Fossil fern leaves (*below right*) are often found in coal.

Most of the insects living 300 million years ago would look familiar today, although many were much larger than similar species that are seen now.

Fossils of *Eryops* show that it was the largest of the early land-living amphibians.

The large amphibian *Eryops* lived in the rainforest – dinosaurs had yet to appear on Earth

Pholiderpeton was another fish-eating amphibian – it lived in the swamp, like an alligator

The jaw of *Eryops* opened downwards, which would have been ideal for catching fish

Ice Age

The plains of northern Europe and northern North America are marked with odd-looking mounds and ridges. The soils contain stones and boulders, some of which have been carried there across hundreds of kilometres. The mountains of northern Europe and Canada are rounded and smoothed, as if worn down and polished by a sculptor. In the high mountains of California and the Alps, however, there are sharp mountain peaks, and lakes are found in the mountain valleys. These features have all been formed by moving ice. For a long period, up until 12,000 years ago, these regions were covered by thick ice sheets. By comparing the land today with how it looked in the past, we can see how ice sheets changed the landscape.

An archaeologist carefully cleans a fossilised mammoth tooth

Under the huge weight of moving ice, the landscape was carved and sculpted

The glacier carried sharp boulders in the ice, which scratched deep grooves in rock surfaces

As the glacier carved the mountains, it left spiky 'alpine' peaks

The thick sheets of ice flowed downhill under gravity, like tongues of frozen liquid

The largest continental ice sheets may have been 3,000 metres thick

Rocks and debris were deposited by the ice sheets, forming hills called drumlins

Huge boulders were picked up by the ice and carried hundreds of kilometres

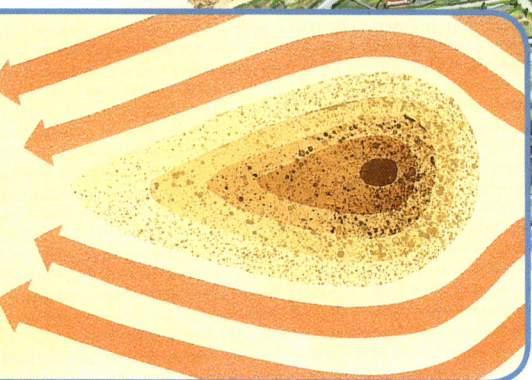

Drumlins

Where ice sheets flowed over and around hard rocks, debris carried by the ice was dropped. The piles of debris rose higher and higher, eventually forming rounded hills called drumlins.

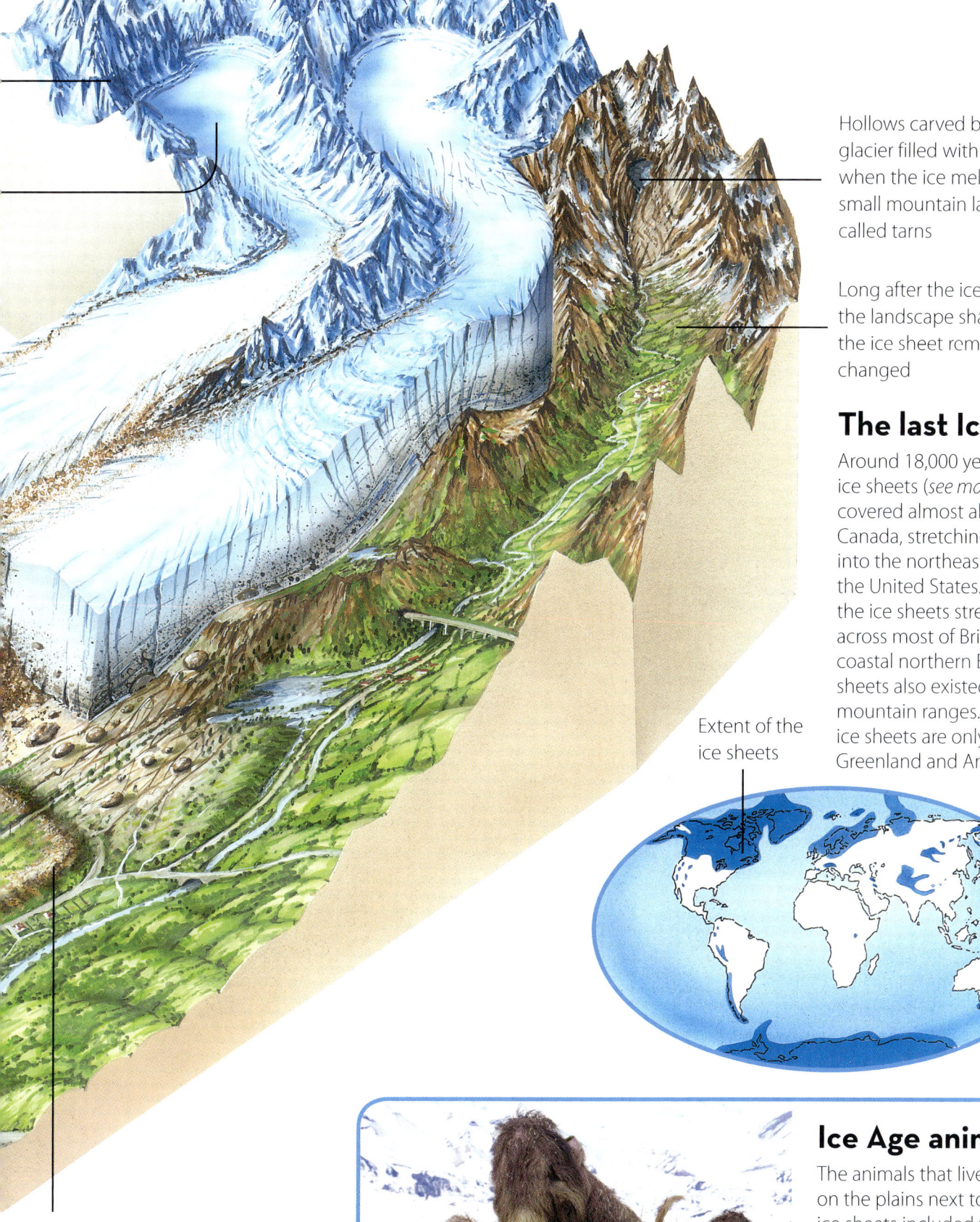

Hollows carved by the glacier filled with water when the ice melted – these small mountain lakes are called tarns

Long after the ice melted, the landscape shaped by the ice sheet remains little changed

The last Ice Age

Around 18,000 years ago, ice sheets (*see map below*) covered almost all of Canada, stretching down into the northeastern part of the United States. In Europe, the ice sheets stretched across most of Britain and coastal northern Europe. Ice sheets also existed in many mountain ranges. Today, ice sheets are only found in Greenland and Antarctica.

Extent of the ice sheets

All over the region once covered by the ice there are moraines: sandy soil filled with stones and boulders

Roads and railways sometimes follow ancient moraine ridges

Ice Age animals

The animals that lived on the plains next to the ice sheets included the mammoth, an extinct relative of the elephant that had a woolly coat. The tusks and bones of mammoths are sometimes found in marshland far away from the ice sheets of today.

Drifting Continents

Since the Earth first formed, its continents have been moving across the globe. Volcanic eruptions and earthquakes are visible signs that the continents crash into and slide past one another. Yet the continents' movements are very slow – just a few centimetres each year. Rocks hold many clues to the speed and direction of the continents' movements over the past hundreds of millions of years. They can tell us about the different climates the land has experienced, as the continents have moved towards or away from the Equator (*see pages 28–29*). The best clues come from evidence of the Earth's magnetism that is trapped in rocks.

200 million years ago, today's continents were part of one supercontinent, called Pangaea

Glossopteris

Echidna

Platypus

Earth's magnetism

The Earth's magnetic field is generated by the movement of hot liquid metal in the centre of the Earth. The lines of magnetic force curl through the Earth, causing the needle of a compass to point north.

Lines of magnetic force

North

When rocks formed 300 million years ago, their magnets pointed north

North

Plants and animals

The fern *glossopteris* once grew widely on the supercontinent of Pangaea. Fossils of the fern have been found in all the lands that made up the supercontinent. Some primitive animals, such as the echidna and platypus, live in Australia, but animals very like them live far away on the continent of South America. They drifted apart on the moving continents, having once lived on the same single supercontinent.

South

The green area shows where glossopteris grew across Pangaea

Around 250 million years ago, Pangaea started to break apart

Magnets in rock

When the hot liquid rock that lies deep in the Earth seeps up onto the Earth's surface through a volcano, it cools and hardens. This causes its iron-rich crystals to solidify and become magnetised. These tiny magnets all point in the direction of the Earth's magnetic field – north. The magnets are all set, forever 'frozen', pointing in the same direction.

If the continents then move, carrying the rocks with them, the 'frozen' magnets may no longer point north. By measuring the direction in which the ancient rock magnets now point, it is possible to know where the rock was when it formed. By looking at many rock magnets, scientists can work out where an entire continent used to be.

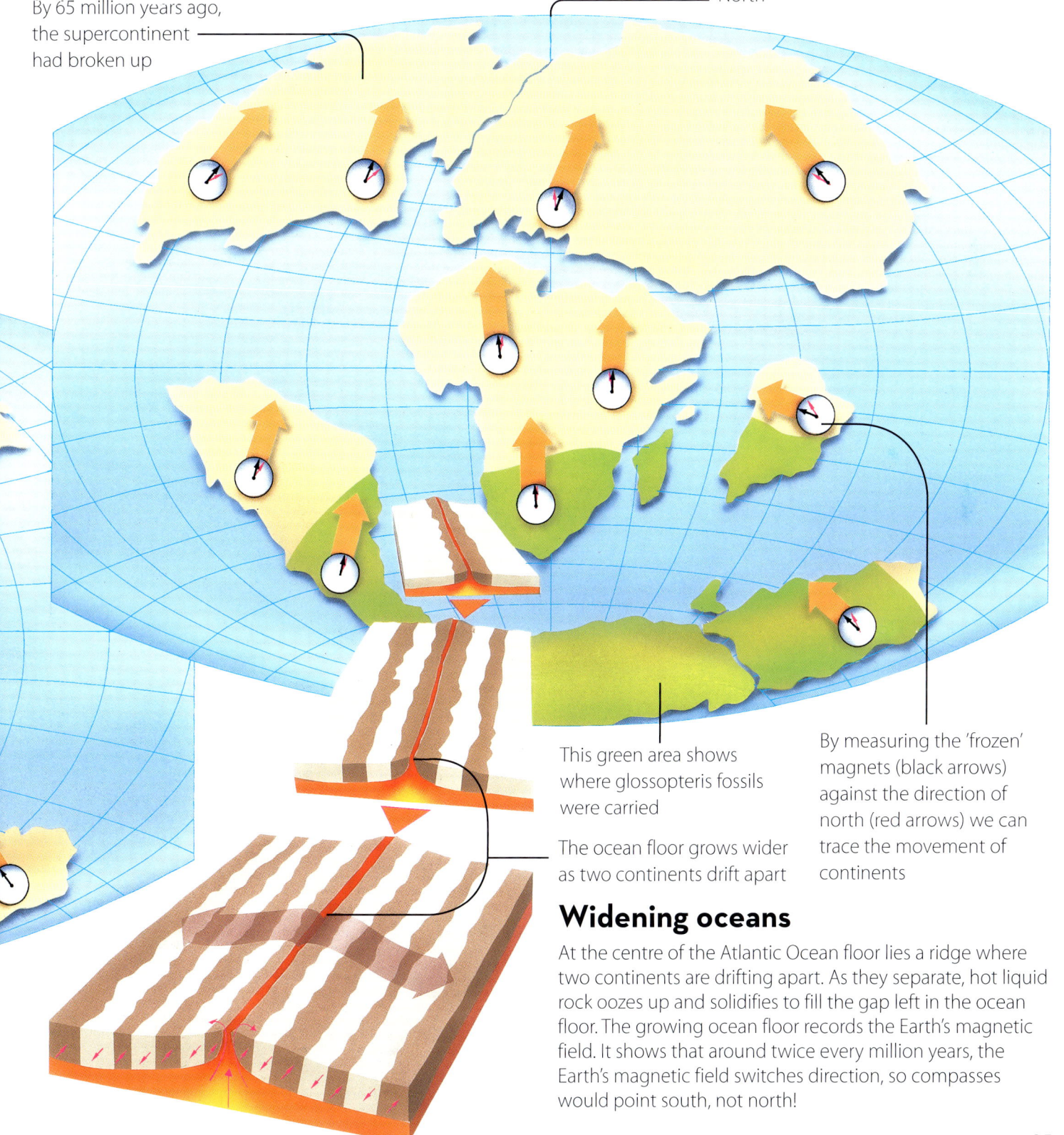

By 65 million years ago, the supercontinent had broken up

North

This green area shows where glossopteris fossils were carried

The ocean floor grows wider as two continents drift apart

By measuring the 'frozen' magnets (black arrows) against the direction of north (red arrows) we can trace the movement of continents

Widening oceans

At the centre of the Atlantic Ocean floor lies a ridge where two continents are drifting apart. As they separate, hot liquid rock oozes up and solidifies to fill the gap left in the ocean floor. The growing ocean floor records the Earth's magnetic field. It shows that around twice every million years, the Earth's magnetic field switches direction, so compasses would point south, not north!

Changing Sea Levels

Where the sea meets the land, there is usually a beach. The breaking waves build banks of sand and shingle, and cut into the land to carve cliffs and rocky platforms. Where a river meets the sea, as the flow of the river slows, sediment carried by the current is dropped and a delta eventually forms. Beaches, cliffs and deltas are features of the sea level. Over thousands of years, the sea level changes. On these pages we look at past sea levels in western Europe and discover the evidence they leave behind, such as ancient beaches, cliffs and deltas.

Flooded villages

Bones and flint remains show that 120,000 years ago prehistoric people camped on the seashores, making flint tools and collecting shellfish.

Three million years ago, the sea reached these mountains

Climate change

Variations in sea level are a result of climate change. Three million years ago, the sea level was high because the Earth's climate was warmer and there were no ice sheets. Sediment laid down at that time, in seas such as the North Sea, is filled with fossils of coral and other warm-water life. A million years later, these seas were covered by ice.

Fossils show that the sea was warm enough for coral reefs to grow

Three million years ago, sea levels were 40 metres higher than they are today

Flooded forests

After the last Ice Age ended 12,000 years ago, the sea level rose rapidly. On many coasts there are drowned forests below the level of today's sea. Sometimes fallen fossil tree trunks record great wind storms that came with the floods. In the sea, fishermen have also found tools and bones from flooded ancient settlements.

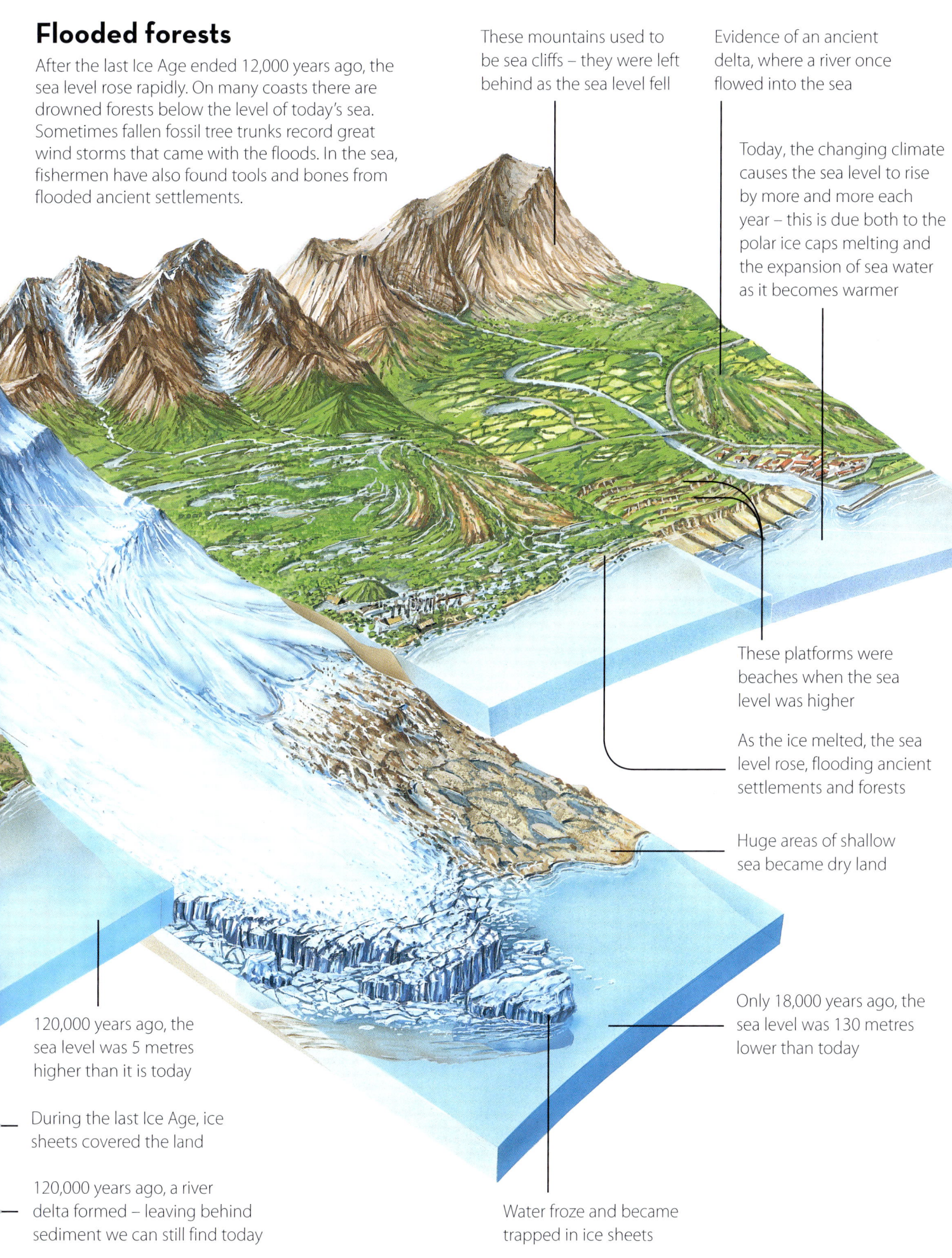

These mountains used to be sea cliffs – they were left behind as the sea level fell

Evidence of an ancient delta, where a river once flowed into the sea

Today, the changing climate causes the sea level to rise by more and more each year – this is due both to the polar ice caps melting and the expansion of sea water as it becomes warmer

These platforms were beaches when the sea level was higher

As the ice melted, the sea level rose, flooding ancient settlements and forests

Huge areas of shallow sea became dry land

120,000 years ago, the sea level was 5 metres higher than it is today

During the last Ice Age, ice sheets covered the land

120,000 years ago, a river delta formed – leaving behind sediment we can still find today

Water froze and became trapped in ice sheets

Only 18,000 years ago, the sea level was 130 metres lower than today

Mountain Building

Mountains rise, are worn down, and eventually disappear. Across the world, there are mountains at different stages of this cycle. The highest are formed where continents collide. The Himalayas, rising to more than 8,000 metres, formed where the Indian land mass crashed into the rest of Asia. Some mountains are volcanoes, forming where molten rock, or magma, from deep inside the Earth pours out at the surface. Others are made from deep-sea sediment that was deposited by rivers and has since been thrust upwards by geological forces. While some mountains are rising, others are slowly being worn away. By studying rocks from mountains at different stages, geologists can build a model of the life cycle of an ancient mountain range.

Snow, ice, wind and rain wear down the rock

Many mountains date from far into prehistory – tens to hundreds of millions of years ago

The rocks at the heart of ancient mountains were once 10,000 to 20,000 metres underground

Where continents collide, layers of rock are squeezed and pushed up

Most mountains begin life as sediments on the ocean floor

Where two continents separate, a ridge appears on the ocean floor

Ocean sediments become layers of rock deep under the sea

Magma pours out onto the ocean floor to fill the widening gap in the ocean floor

Squashed, folded rocks rise up out of the ocean to form mountains

Where continents collide, one continent may be pushed down beneath the Earth's surface

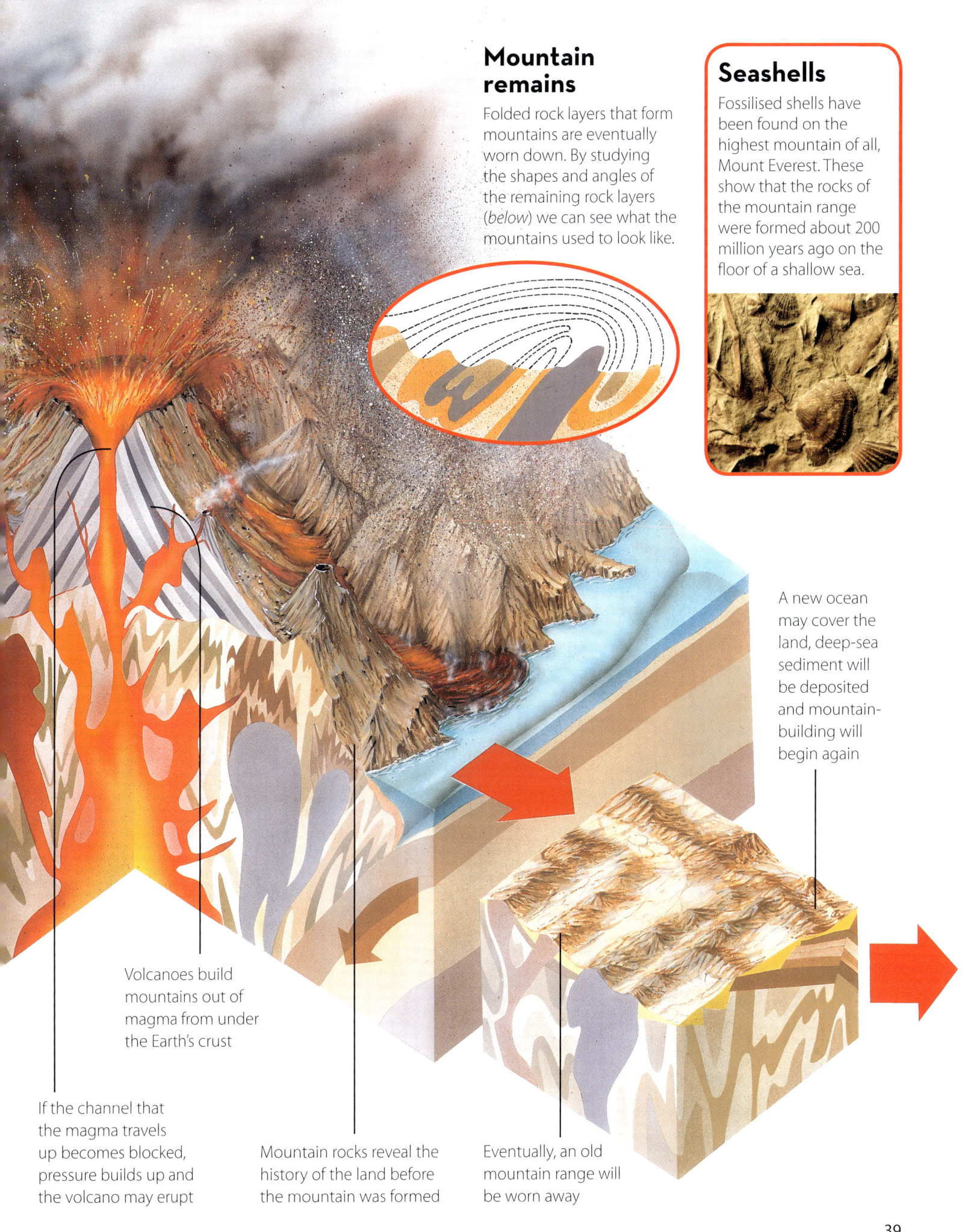

Mountain remains

Folded rock layers that form mountains are eventually worn down. By studying the shapes and angles of the remaining rock layers (*below*) we can see what the mountains used to look like.

Seashells

Fossilised shells have been found on the highest mountain of all, Mount Everest. These show that the rocks of the mountain range were formed about 200 million years ago on the floor of a shallow sea.

A new ocean may cover the land, deep-sea sediment will be deposited and mountain-building will begin again

Volcanoes build mountains out of magma from under the Earth's crust

If the channel that the magma travels up becomes blocked, pressure builds up and the volcano may erupt

Mountain rocks reveal the history of the land before the mountain was formed

Eventually, an old mountain range will be worn away

Early Peoples

At the same time that northern Europe was covered in ice sheets, there were forests in the river valleys of south-western France. Beneath soils of wind-driven dust and river sediment, archaeologists have found traces of the people who lived in this region between 15,000 and 10,000 BC. These Magdalenian people were hunters, living off the large herds of animals that moved through the valleys. Food was plentiful and the people had time to create new tools and even make ornamental objects. The Magdalenian people have left many clues as to how they lived. By excavating sites across the region, we have been able to build up a picture of their lives.

Wall paintings

The people of this region painted pictures of the animals they hunted, such as this bison, along the walls of caves. Forms of natural mineral dye, such as red ochre, were used as paint.

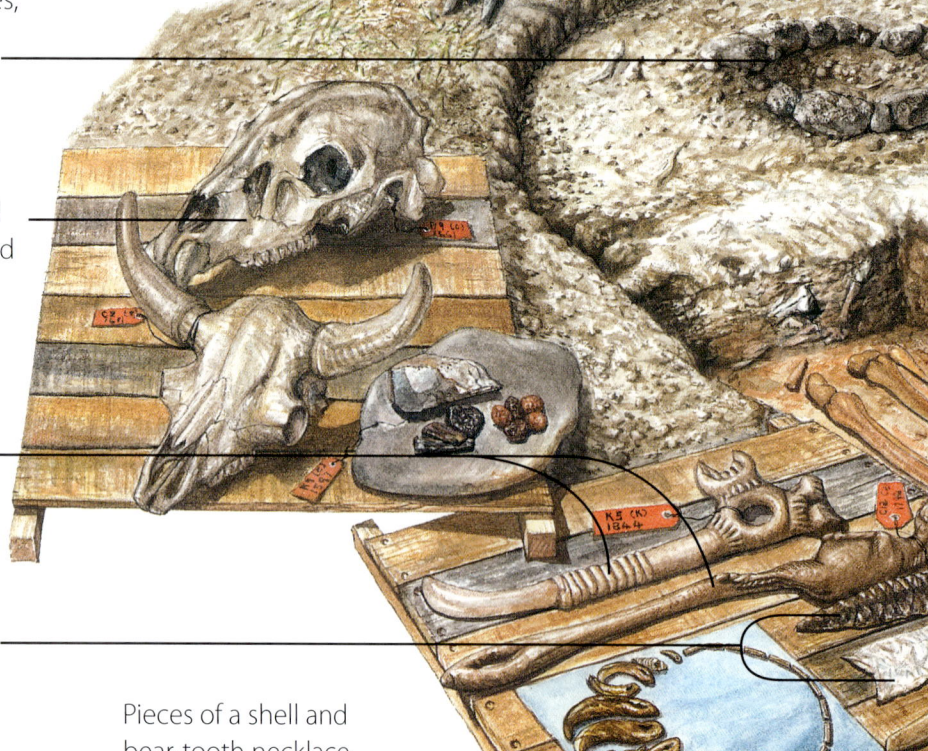

The hearth of a fire leaves a patch of burnt bones, scorched stones and charcoal fragments

Excavated remains have been assembled on boards and labelled

Mammoth and antler bone were carved into tools

Flint arrows and spearheads were fitted onto wooden sticks, which have since rotted away

Pieces of a shell and bear-tooth necklace have been found and gathered together

Needles made from ivory (mammoth tusks) were used to sew skins together to make clothes

Clues to a lifestyle

Fossils from the site of the Magdalenian people show they hunted herds of bison and reindeer, and also fished. Their food was cooked over a fire. They probably lived in communities and exchanged goods with other members of their tribe. From their carvings we can tell that they communicated with other tribes across central Europe.

Objects found at their burial places seem to show they believed the dead would live again in this, or another, world. The Magdalenians were among the first humans to make art objects. Items such as carved animals may have had symbolic or spiritual meaning to the people who made them.

Skins for warmth

The Magdalenian people lived only a few hundred kilometres south of the ice sheet, so their environment was not very warm. Animal skins (*below*) were used for clothing, as well as for lining their tent-like homes.

Bones reveal the range of animals that were eaten

Stones around a saucer-shaped hole mark the site of a tent-like home

This bison was carved out of a reindeer antler

This sitting bear was carved out of soft stone

This hunter was buried in a special ceremony, surrounded by weapons and tools

Radiocarbon dating of the bones shows that this man and the animals are from the same period

Reconstructing Faces

What were the first human beings like? The only remains that archaeologists have found are fragments of fossil bones and skulls. Bones of early humans known as *Australopithecus Afarensis* have been found in sediment laid down in eastern Africa. We can tell the age of these bones from the volcanic ash sediment in which they were found. The sediment layers were dated using the potassium-argon radioisotope technique (*see pages 16–17*) and found to be around four million years old.

Fossils of the legs of a female *Australopithecus* show that these ancient humans walked upright. An adult female stood around 1.5 metres tall. After piecing together fragments of the skull, we can also see what the face of this prehistoric human looked like. On these pages we see the processes involved in the traditional manual reconstruction of a skull, and the modelling of the face and head.

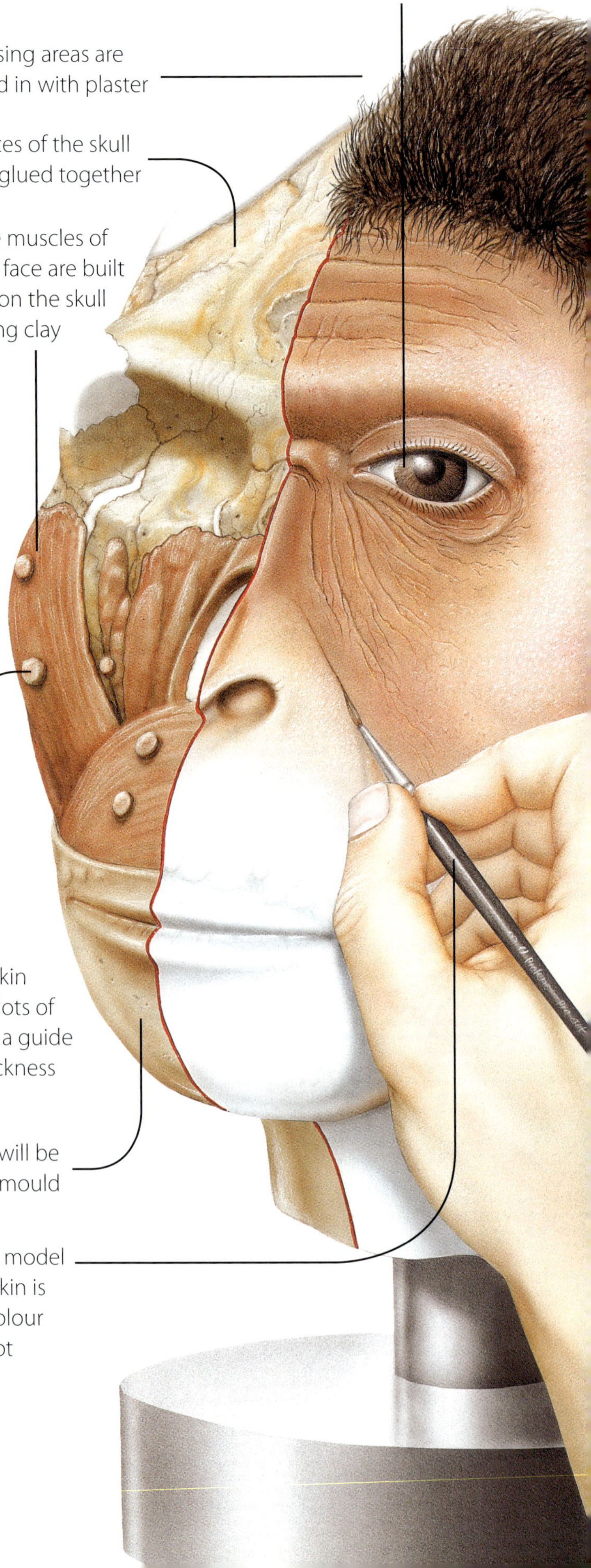

Computer faces

Computers are also used to reconstruct faces. The skull is scanned by a laser so that its exact shape can be seen on a computer screen. Muscles and skin are added onto the image electronically. Different skin tones and hair length or colour can be tested too.

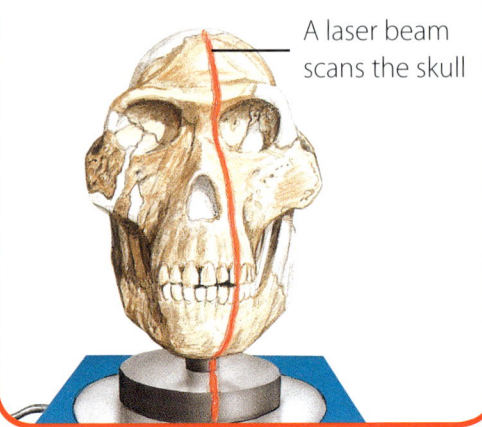

A laser beam scans the skull

Glass eyes of the correct size are inserted into the eye sockets

Missing areas are filled in with plaster

Pieces of the skull are glued together

The muscles of the face are built up on the skull using clay

When the clay skin layer is added, dots of clay are used as a guide for the right thickness

The clay model will be used to make a mould

The hard plastic model is painted. The skin is recreated in a colour typical of this hot region of Africa

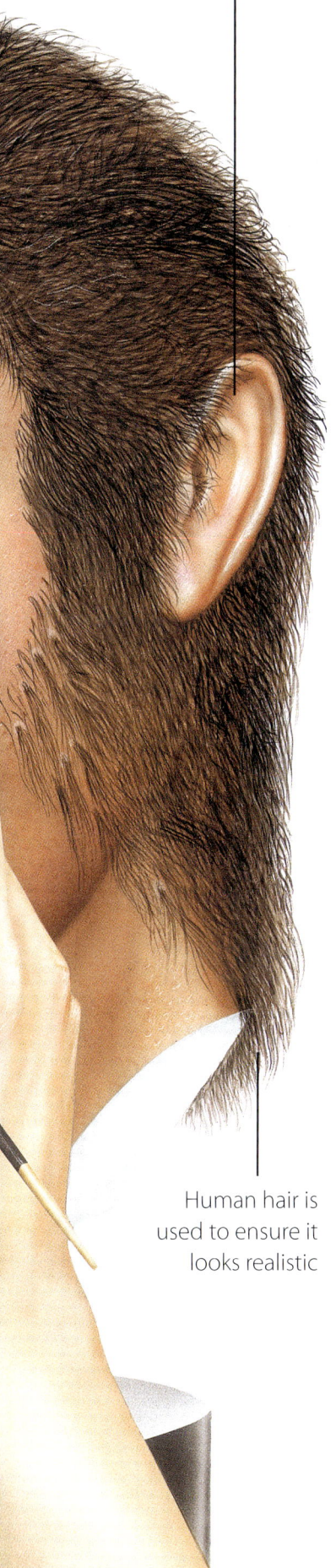

Ears, like the nose, are sculpted into shapes based on apes' and human features

Human hair is used to ensure it looks realistic

The clay model

Fossil skulls are rarely complete. Fragile bones, such as those of the nose, tend to splinter and are lost. So the first job is to repair the skull. Pieces are glued together and missing sections filled with plaster.

By looking at the skull, and at the muscles on faces of modern human beings, scientists can work out where the muscles would have been. The face muscles are formed on the skull using clay (**I**). Careful measurements of the skull are also taken to decide how big the nose and eyes should be.

For the skin of *Australopithecus*, a simple layer of clay, two to three millimetres deep, is added. This final layer is shaped and sculpted with wrinkles and lines to make it more realistic.

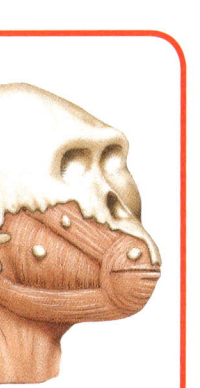

The plastic copy

When the clay model is complete, rubber is poured over it to make a mould. When the mould is ready, plastic is poured into it and left to set. The rubber mould is then peeled off, leaving a rigid plastic copy of the clay model (**2**). The clay model, containing the precious bone, can be returned to the museum. The plastic copy is passed over to the artist.

The completed reconstruction

The model is brought to life with paint, glass eyes and hair (**3**). The amount of hair on the *Autralopithecus* can only be guessed at, although the hair on modern humans and living apes can be used as a guide. The amount of hair added changes the appearance greatly.

Our ancestors

Archaeologists have created a timeline of human evolution by studying the skulls they have found and the times when those humans would have lived. Notably, the brain size increases as evolution progresses. You can see this by the changing shape of the skull, which allows more space for the brain.

Sahelanthropus tchadensis (7–6 million years ago)

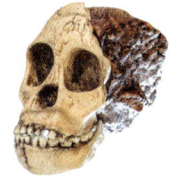

Australopithecus africanus (4 million years ago)

Homo erectus (1.8–1.5 million years ago)

Homo neanderthaensis (230,000 years ago)

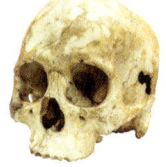

Homo sapiens (195,000 years ago)

Early Beliefs

Much of what we know about prehistoric peoples comes from the many monuments they left behind. Some of these were built as burial chambers, and others were used for ceremonial purposes. Among the most mysterious monuments is Stonehenge, built of 162 blocks of stone on a plateau in southern England. Most of our discoveries about the monument and the people who built it have come from excavations at the site. We know that some of the stones were quarried hundreds of kilometres away, and that it probably took hundreds of men to haul just one of them. The immense effort involved suggests the people had very strong reasons for building Stonehenge.

Why was Stonehenge built?

The Sun aligns with certain stones at the summer and winter solstice (the longest and shortest days of the year). The Sun also aligns with stones at the equinoxes (days of equal day and night). So it is possible that Stonehenge was used as an astronomical calendar, showing when to plant crops or observe festivals.

Stonehenge

The picture below shows three stages in the life of Stonehenge: its building (*below*), its completion (*centre*) and the ruins left today (*right*). When complete, Stonehenge comprised a ring of upright stones with a continuous roof of lintels (flat stones laid across the upright ones). There was an inner horseshoe-shaped ring of five pairs of separate uprights, each pair with its own curved lintel. Inside both rings stood smaller stones (bluestones). The monument was in the middle of a circular bank surrounded by a ditch, and a broad avenue led to the site.

The lintels were perhaps lifted on platforms

Poles were probably used to help lift the stones into place

When complete, Stonehenge probably looked like this

Stonehenge was built at different stages in prehistory

The oldest radiocarbon date measured at the site shows that the bank and ditch were cut around 3000 BC

The stones were carved to fit tightly against each other

The giant inner stones weigh up to 45 tonnes each

Burial mounds

In the region around Stonehenge there are many burial mounds, known as barrows. They were built at the same time as the great stone circle. To explore barrows, a series of trenches are dug. The barrow shown here has a passageway and several burial chambers where human bones were found.

Some of the stones are still standing today

People still gather at Stonehenge at the winter solstice in December – the year's shortest day with the fewest hours of daylight – to celebrate the return of light and rebirth of the land with the coming spring.

In June, the summer solstice – the day of the year with the most hours of daylight – is celebrated to give thanks for the power of the Sun and the harvest it provides, and for the balance that the seasons bring to our planet.

The outer circle was built around 2500 BC, using stones quarried about 20 miles (30 kilometres) away

The bluestones were brought over 130 miles (210 kilometres), from south Wales, in around 2300 to 2200 BC

Index